Keto

Vegetarian

Cookbook

30 Days meal guide for

Beginners

FOREWORD

Congratulations on taking the first step towards a healthy lifestyle!

This book presents a 30-day meal plan for those who want to start on a keto vegetarian diet. We have made all efforts to make the recipes in this book "beginner friendly", with ingredients that are quite accessible and with as little preparation time as possible. We realize how difficult and overwhelming it can be to change your eating habits, and we wanted to make this journey as easy for you as possible.

Take note that we always refer to a keto vegetarian diet as more than just a diet, but a lifestyle. Embracing a healthy lifestyle means letting it influence all areas of your life – from having a healthy diet, to getting regular exercise, and getting enough sleep every day. It takes a conscious decision and constant effort to change how you do things, and to achieve physical, mental, and spiritual health.

We encourage that you don't think of a healthy "diet" as something you will only do for 30 days. What we provide in this book is an opportunity for you to take the first steps towards transforming your lifestyle and becoming a healthier version of you.

For those who are not new to the keto vegetarian lifestyle, we hope that this book opens up and expands your dining choices. We have made an effort to come up with recipes that are not only healthy, but also taste great. The point that we are trying to make is that you don't have to feel deprived when you're on a keto vegetarian diet. After all, life is too short to not enjoy.

"I really recommend that before trying a ketogenic diet or any kind of diet please see a physician first to check if it will be safe for you. I will not be held responsible for any health problems you may encounter due to improper usage of the diet" Again, thank you for buying our book. Best of luck!

Erin Mira

TABLE OF CONTENTS

INTRODUCTION

WHAT IS A VEGETARIAN?

A vegetarian is someone who doesn't eat meat, and mostly eats foods that come from plants, like grains, fruits, vegetables, and nuts. Some stricter vegetarians avoid more than just meat. They also avoid animal products, which are nonmeat foods that come from animals. Some examples would be milk (from cows) and eggs (from chickens).

Types of Vegetarians

Lacto-ovo vegetarian: eats no meat, but will eat dairy products (milk, butter, cheese) and eggs; this is the most common type of vegetarian diet

Lacto vegetarian: eats dairy products but does not eat eggs

Ovo-vegetarian: eats eggs, but not dairy products

Vegan: does not eat eggs, dairy products, or any other food derived from animals

What is a keto vegetarian diet?

 Simply put, a keto vegetarian diet restricts all forms of animal meat while restricting carbohydrate intake. The goal of this diet is to speed up weight loss by stimulating fat burning. Aside from promoting a better overall health, having a keto vegetarian diet is also an exhibit of disapproval of animal cruelty and abuse that runs rampant in the production of food derived from animal meat.

A traditional keto diet focuses on a meal plan that is very high in fat, very low in carbohydrates, and a moderate level of protein. The keto vegetarian diet does not stray from this general template but eliminates animal meat from the equation. As a

general rule of thumb a keto vegetarian diet should be broken down as less than 5 percent carbohydrates, 15 to 20 percent protein, and 75 to 80 percent fat.

What are the benefits of a ketogenic diet to you?

1. Weight loss

As you cut your CARBOHYDRATE intake, you deprive your body of glucose, which is the main source of energy for all cells in the body. At this state, the tendency of your body is to find another source of fuel to sustain activity. This is where ketones come to the rescue!

During diet where very little carbohydrate is eaten, the body first pulls stored glucose from the liver and temporarily breaks down muscle to release glucose. If this continues for 3-4 days and stored glucose is fully depleted, blood levels of a hormone called insulin decrease, and the body begins to use fat as its primary fuel. The liver produces ketone bodies from fat, which can be used in the absence of glucose.

ATTENTION!

Excessive ketone bodies can produce a dangerously toxic level of acid in the blood, called ketoacidosis. During ketoacidosis, the kidneys begin to excrete ketone bodies along with body water in the urine, causing some fluid-related weight loss. Ketoacidosis most often occurs in individuals with type 1 diabetes because they do not produce insulin, a hormone that prevents the overproduction of ketones. However, in few rare cases, ketoacidosis has been reported to occur in non-diabetic individuals following a prolonged very low carbohydrate diet. This means that it is important that you ask your doctor for advice before you start this kind of diet.

As the old saying goes, "EVERYTHING IN MODERATION."

2. Reduced risk for Type 2 Diabetes

The process of burning fat provides more benefits than simply helping us to shed extra weight — it also helps control the release of hormones like insulin, which plays a role in the development of diabetes and other health problems. When we eat carbohydrates, insulin is released as a reaction to elevated blood glucose (an increase in sugar circulating in our blood) and insulin levels rise. Insulin is a "storage hormone" that signals cells to store as much available energy as possible, initially as glycogen (aka stored carbohydrates in our muscles) and then as body fat.

The ketogenic diet works by eliminating carbohydrates from the diet and keeping the body's carbohydrate stores almost empty, therefore preventing too much insulin from being released following food consumption and creating normal blood sugar levels. This can help reverse "insulin resistance," which is the underlying problem contributing to diabetes symptoms. In studies, low-carb diets have shown benefits for improving blood pressure, postprandial glycemia and insulin secretion. (7) Therefore, diabetics on insulin should contact their medical provider prior to starting a ketogenic diet; however, as insulin dosages may need to be adjusted.

3. Reduced risk of heart disease

The keto diet can reduce the risk of heart disease markers, including high cholesterol and triglycerides. In fact, the keto diet is unlikely to negatively impact your cholesterol levels despite being so high in fat. Moreover, it's capable of lowering cardiovascular disease risk factors, especially in those who are obese.

For instance, one study found that adhering to the ketogenic diet for 24 weeks resulted in decreased levels of triglycerides, LDL cholesterol and blood glucose in a significant percentage of patients, while at the same time increasing the level of HDL cholesterol.

4. Help protect against Cancer

Certain studies suggest that ketogenic diets may "starve" cancer cells. A highly processed, pro-inflammatory, low-nutrient diet can feed cancer cells causing them to proliferate. What's the connection between a high-sugar diet and cancer? The regular cells found in our bodies are able to use fat for energy, but it's believed that cancer cells cannot metabolically shift to use fat rather than glucose.

There are several medical studies — such as two conducted by the Department of Radiation Oncology at the Holden Comprehensive Cancer Center for the University of Iowa, and the National Institutes of Health's National Institute of Neurological Disorders and Stroke — that show the ketogenic diet is an effective treatment for cancer and other serious health problems.

Therefore, a diet that eliminates excess refined sugar and other processed carbohydrates may be effective in reducing or fighting cancer. It's not a coincidence that some of the best cancer-fighting foods are on the ketogenic diet food list.

5. Fight brain disease and neurological disorders

Over the past century, ketogenic diets have also been used to treat and even help reverse neurological disorders and cognitive impairments, including epilepsy and Alzheimer's symptoms. Research shows that cutting off glucose levels with a very low-carb diet makes your body produce ketones for fuel. This change can help to reverse neurological disorders and cognitive impairment. The brain is able to use this alternative source of energy instead of the cellular energy pathways that aren't functioning normally in patients with brain disorders.

For example, clinical improvement was observed in Alzheimer's patients fed a ketogenic diet, and this was marked by improved mitochondrial function. In fact, a European Journal of Clinical Nutrition study pointed to emerging data that suggested the therapeutic use of ketogenic diets for multiple neurological disorders beyond epilepsy and Alzheimer's, including headaches, neurotrauma, Parkinson's disease, sleep disorders, brain cancer, autism, and multiple sclerosis.

The report goes on to say that while these various diseases are clearly different from each other, the ketogenic diet appears to be so effective for neurological problems because of its "neuroprotective effect" — as the keto appears to correct abnormalities in cellular energy usage, which is a common characteristic in many neurological disorders.

Researchers believe that the ketogenic diet can also help patients with schizophrenia to normalize the pathophysiological processes that are causing symptoms like delusions, hallucinations, lack of restraint and unpredictable behavior. One study found that the ketogenic diet leads to elevated concentrations of kynurenic acid (KYNA) in the hippocampus and striatum, which promotes neuroactive activity. Some studies even point to the elimination of gluten under the ketogenic diet as a possible reason for improved symptoms, as researchers observed that patients with schizophrenia tended to eat more carbohydrates immediately before a psychotic episode.

Although the exact role of the ketogenic diet in mental and brain disorders is unclear, there has been proof of its efficacy in patients with schizophrenia. And, to boot, the ketogenic diet works to reverse many conditions that develop as a side effect of conventional medications for brain disorders, like weight gain, type 2 diabetes, and cardiovascular risks. More research is needed to understand the role of the ketogenic diet in treating or improving schizophrenia, as the currently available studies are either animal studies or case studies, but the benefits of this high-fat, low-carbohydrate diet in neurology is promising.

6. Live longer

There's even evidence that a low-carb, high-fat diet helps you live longer, compared to a low-fat diet. In a study by the medical journal The Lancet that studied more than 135,000 adults from 18 countries, high carbohydrate intake was associated with higher risk of total mortality, whereas total fat and individual types of fat were related to lower total mortality. Total fat and types of fat were not associated with cardiovascular disease, myocardial infarction or cardiovascular disease mortality.

In fact, saturated fat intake had an inverse association with the risk for suffering from a stroke, meaning the more saturated fat included in someone's diet, the more protection against having a stroke they seemed to have.

What are the challenges of adopting a keto vegetarian diet?

Aside from the heavy restrictions imposed by this diet, the lack of any meat or grains intake may lead to deficiency of specific nutrients, vitamins, and minerals. Vitamin B12, iron, and

omega-3 fatty acids are largely obtained from animal products, with fish being particularly high in omega-3. Zinc, a common antioxidant, is also commonly derived from meat and poultry. Calcium, magnesium, and Vitamin D, compounds that are vital to bone health are commonly sourced from grains and dairy products. Although a keto vegetarian diet has loads of benefits, it also has its limitations which may results in adverse health effects. If you are unsure if a keto vegetarian diet is right for you, the best recommendation is to consult a qualified physician. It may also be a good idea to take the transition slowly and see how your body will respond.

What can I eat and cannot eat under a keto vegetarian diet?

In preparing a meal plan for a keto vegetarian diet, it is often easier to start by listing down the foods that you avoid to eat or be responsible on the amount when you eat This list includes:

1.   Grains – rice, corn, oats, cereal, wheat, bran
2.   Legumes – peas, lentils, beans, chickpeas
3.   Fruit – apples, bananas, mangoes, oranges
4.   Sugar – honey, maple syrup, agave
5.   Tubers – yams, sweet potatoes, potatoes
6.   Animal meat – poultry, fish, pork, beef, lamb, seafood

The restriction against meat is particularly challenging, as it acts as the primary source of protein for the traditional keto diet. However, a keto vegetarian diet does not have to be so limited.

Below is the list of foods recommended for a keto vegetarian diet:

1. Eggs
2. Avocado
3. High fat dairy – butter, high fat cream and milk,
    different types of cheeses
4. Nuts and seeds – almonds, walnuts, sunflower seeds, pumpkin seeds, flaxseed
5. Coconut products – coconut milk, coconut flour, desiccated coconut
6. Soy products – tofu, soy milk,
7. Leafy greens – spinach, collard greens, cabbage, lettuce
8. Sweeteners – Stevia, erythritol, monk fruit
9. Fats and oils – olive oil, sesame oil, coconut oil, butter, ghee
10. Above ground vegetables – zucchini, cauliflower, broccoli

The Recipes

DAY 1

Meal	Recipe	Calories
Breakfast	Scrambled Eggs with Spinach and Feta + Spinach Cucumber Smoothie	369 + 244
Lunch	Low-Carb Fried Eggplant	822
Dinner	Zoodles with Parmesan and Walnuts	475

Scrambled Eggs with Spinach and Feta

INGREDIENTS	Fats	Proteins	Carbs
2 eggs	8.37 g	11.05 g	0.63 g
1 cup spinach	0.12 g	0.86 g	1.09 g
1/4 cup feta cheese	7.98 g	5.33 g	1.53 g
1/8 cup fat-free cream	0.42 g	0.79 g	2.72 g
1 tbsp. olive oil (for frying)	13.5 g	0 g	0 g

Nutrition Facts

Amount per 199 g
1 serving (7 oz)

Calories   369
  From fat   270

Amount	% Daily Value*	Amount	% Daily Value*
Total Fat 30.4g	47%	Total Carbohydrates 6g	2%
Saturated 10.5g	52%	Dietary Fiber 1g	3%
Trans Fat 0g		Sugars 4g	
Cholesterol 362mg	121%	Protein 18g	36%
Sodium 523mg	22%		
Calcium 29% • Iron 15%		Vitamin A 69% • Vitamin C 14%	

* Percent Daily Values are based on 2000 calorie diet. Your Daily Values may be higher or lower depending on your calorie needs.

Directions

1.   Crack open 2 eggs and whisk in a small bowl until thoroughly combined.

2.   Mix the fat-free cream with the eggs. Whisk the mixture until slightly airy.

3.   Brush a frying pan lightly with olive oil. Start heating the pan over a stove at low heat. When the pan is hot enough, pour in the egg mixture.

4.   Cook on one side for 2 to 3 minutes, or until the bottom has started to set. At this point, mix in the spinach.

5.   Start stirring the egg mixture continuously to keep the scrambled eggs creamy.

6.   Allow the spinach to cook and wilt a little for about 1 minute.

7.   Break up the feta cheese into small chunks and distribute evenly over the scrambled eggs.

8.   Continue cooking until the eggs are done to your liking.

9.   Season with salt and pepper, if desired.

Did you know?

Spinach is in fact, one of the most nutritious vegetables. It's high in iron, which helps build red blood cells. Red blood cells carry oxygen through the body and provide energy. Spinach is also a good source of vitamin A, vitamin K, and vitamin

Spinach Cucumber Smoothie

INGREDIENTS	Fats	Proteins	Carbs
2 cups spinach	0.23 g	1.72 g	2.18 g
1/2 cup cucumber, cubed	0.10 g	0.35 g	1.29 g
1 cup coconut milk	24.1 g	2.28 g	3.18 g
12 drops Stevia	0 g	0 g	1 g
7 ice cubes	-	-	-

Nutrition Facts	Amount	% Daily Value*	Amount	% Daily Value*
Amount per 234 g	Total Fat 24.4g	38%	Total Carbohydrates 8g	3%
1 serving (8.2 oz)	Saturated 21.4g	107%	Dietary Fiber 2g	7%
	Trans Fat 0g		Sugars 1g	
Calories 244	Cholesterol 0mg	0%	Protein 4g	9%
From fat 205	Sodium 63mg	3%		
	Calcium 9% • Iron 31%		Vitamin A 113% • Vitamin C 33%	

* Percent Daily Values are based on 2000 calorie diet. Your Daily Values may be higher or lower depending on your calorie needs.

Directions

1.   In a blender, mix in the spinach, Stevia, coconut milk, and ice cubes. Blend until smooth.

2.   Top with cubed cucumber and serve.

Did you know?

Cucumbers contain insoluble and soluble fiber that helps you feel full and also lowers bad cholesterol in your body

Low-Carb Fried Eggplant

INGREDIENTS	Fats	Proteins	Carbs
1 small eggplant (approx. 0.1 kg)	0.10 g	0.54 g	3.22 g
1/8 cup almond flour	6.19 g	2.62 g	2.67 g
1/2tbsp. grated parmesan cheese	0.13 g	1 g	1 g
2 eggs	8.37 g	11.05 g	0.63 g
1/2 tsp Italian seasoning	0 g	0.06 g	0.81 g
5tbsp. olive oil	67.5 g	0 g	0 g

Nutrition Facts

Amount per 227 g
1 serving (8 oz)

Calories 822
From fat 726

	Amount	% Daily Value*	Amount	% Daily Value*
	Total Fat 82.3g	127%	Total Carbohydrates 8g	3%
	Saturated 12.6g	63%	Dietary Fiber 3g	14%
	Trans Fat 0.1g		Sugars 3g	
	Cholesterol 328mg	109%	Protein 15g	31%
	Sodium 257mg	11%		
	Calcium 11% • Iron 15%		Vitamin A 11% • Vitamin C 2%	

* Percent Daily Values are based on 2000 calorie diet. Your Daily Values may be higher or lower depending on your calorie needs.

Directions

1.   Combine the almond flour, grated parmesan cheese, and Italian season in a large plate. Set aside.

2.   Break the eggs into a small bowl and whisk until thoroughly mixed. Set aside.

3.   Slice the eggplant lengthwise into 1/4-inch slices. You may leave the skin on. Pat the slices dry using a paper towel.

4.   Heat the olive oil in a frying pan over medium heat.

5.   Dip each piece of eggplant into the egg mixture and coat lightly with the breading mixture. Make sure that each eggplant slice has been completely covered.

6.   Fry the eggplant slices until the coating is golden brown. You may fry several pieces at the same time, but make sure that the pan does not get overcrowded.

7.   After frying, drain the excess oil over paper towels.

8.   Season with salt and pepper before serving, if desired.

Did you know?
Salting eggplant will reduce the amount of oil absorbed in cooking.

Zoodles with Parmesan And Walnuts

INGREDIENTS	Fats	Proteins	Carbs
1 large zucchini (approx. 0.3 kg)	0.06 g	0.43 g	0.50 g
1/4 cup ricotta cheese	4.18 g	3.63 g	0.98 g
1/4 cup chopped macadamia nuts	6.06 g	0.63 g	1.11 g

1 cup raw radicchio	0.1 g	0.57 g	1.79 g
1/8 cup olive oil	28.1 g	0 g	0 g
1 tbsp. lemon juice	0.02 g	0.03 g	0.52 g
1 tsp chopped garlic	0.01 g	0.18 g	0.93 g
1/4 cup Greek yogurt	0.23 g	6.11 g	2.16 g
1/8 cup shredded cheddar	4.97 g	3.53 g	0.2 g

Nutrition Facts

Amount per 209 g
1 serving (7.4 oz)

Calories 475
From fat 384

Amount	% Daily Value*	Amount	% Daily Value*
Total Fat 43.7g	67%	**Total Carbohydrates** 8g	3%
Saturated 10.5g	52%	Dietary Fiber 1g	5%
Trans Fat 0.2g		Sugars 3g	
Cholesterol 34mg	11%	**Protein** 15g	30%
Sodium 154mg	6%		
Calcium 26% • **Iron** 6%		**Vitamin A** 8% • **Vitamin C** 21%	

* Percent Daily Values are based on 2000 calorie diet. Your Daily Values may be higher or lower depending on your calorie needs.

Directions

1.   Slice the zucchini into noodles using a spiralizer. If you don't have a spiralizer, a mandolin slicer will do to slice it into thin strips.

2.   Shred or slice the radicchio into bite-sized strips.

3.	Mix together the spiralized zucchini, radicchio, ricotta cheese, shredded cheddar cheese, Greek yogurt, and macadamia nuts.

4.	For the dressing, mix together the olive oil, lemon juice, and chopped garlic. Add a pinch of salt and pepper.

5.	Add the dressing and salad and toss thoroughly. Serve immediately. Enjoy!

Did you know?

70% of Parmesan is made up of nutrients: rich in proteins, vitamins and minerals, it is the perfect food for children and those who practice sports

DAY 2

Meal	Recipe	Calories
Breakfast	Keto Pumpkin Pancakes	551
Lunch	Cauliflower Spinach Bowl	499
Dinner	Broccoli and Cheese Fritters	932

Keto Pumpkin Pancakes

INGREDIENTS	Fats	Proteins	Carbs
1/4 cup pumpkin puree	0.17 g	0.67 g	4.96 g
2 eggs	0.11 g	7.19 g	0.48 g
2 tbsp. coconut flour	5.16 g	0.55 g	1.89 g
1/4 tsp cinnamon powder	0.01 g	0.03 g	0.56 g
1/4 tsp. vanilla extract	0 g	0 g	0.14 g
2 tbsp. coconut oil (for frying)	27.2 g	0 g	0 g
2 tbsp. butter	23.04 g	0.24 g	0.02 g

Nutrition Facts

Amount per 193 g
1 serving (6.8 oz)

Calories 551
From fat 483

Amount	% Daily Value*	Amount	% Daily Value*
Total Fat 55.7g	86%	Total Carbohydrates 8g	3%
Saturated 42.8g	214%	Dietary Fiber 4g	14%
Trans Fat 1g		Sugars 3g	
Cholesterol 61mg	20%	Protein 9g	17%
Sodium 298mg	12%		
Calcium 4% • Iron 7%		Vitamin A 205% • Vitamin C 5%	

* Percent Daily Values are based on 2000 calorie diet. Your Daily Values may be higher or lower depending on your calorie needs.

Directions

1.   Whisk together the pumpkin puree and eggs in a large bowl.

2.   Whisk in the cinnamon powder and vanilla extract.

3.   Gradually add in the coconut flour while continuing whisking. Mix until just after all the lumps are gone.

4.   Heat coconut oil on a frying pan at medium heat.

5.   When the frying pan is hot enough, add the pancake batter one tablespoon at a time.

6.   Cook one side until bubbles start appearing at the surface. Flip and cook the other side. Cook until both sides are a golden brown color.

7.   Serve pancakes with butter.

Did you know?
September 26th is National Pancake Day.

Cauliflower Spinach Bowl

INGREDIENTS	Fats	Proteins	Carbs
3/4 cups cauliflower, chopped	0.22 g	1.54 g	3.99 g
1 cup spinach	0.12 g	0.86 g	1.09 g
1/4 cup almonds, chopped	0.15 g	0.06 g	0.06 g
0.25 tbsp garlic, chopped	0.01 g	0.13 g	0.69 g

1/2 cup cilantro leaves	0.04 g	0.17 g	0.29 g
2 tbsp. olive oil	27 g	0 g	0 g
1/2 tbsp. sunflower seeds	1.13 g	0.46 g	0.44 g
1/2 cup ricotta cheese	15.97 g	13.85 g	3.74

Nutrition Facts

Amount per 273 g
1 serving (9.6 oz)

Calories 499
From fat 393

Amount	% Daily Value*	Amount	% Daily Value*
Total Fat 44.6g	69%	Total Carbohydrates 10g	3%
Saturated 14.2g	71%	Dietary Fiber 3g	11%
Trans Fat 0g		Sugars 2g	
Cholesterol 63mg	21%	Protein 17g	34%
Sodium 156mg	7%		
Calcium 31% • Iron 12%		Vitamin A 78% • Vitamin C 83%	

* Percent Daily Values are based on 2000 calorie diet. Your Daily Values may be higher or lower depending on your calorie needs.

Directions

1.   Pre-heat your oven to 375 F. Spread the almonds evenly over a small baking tray and bake until golden brown, about 7 to 10 minutes Set aside.

2.   Separate the cauliflower into florets and place into a food processor. Pulse repeatedly until you obtain a rice-like texture.

3.   In a separate pan, heat 1 tbsp. of olive oil over medium heat. Add in the cauliflower rice and chopped garlic. Cook while stirring occasionally. The cauliflower rice is done when it has turned golden brown. Season with salt and pepper.

4.   To the same pan as the cauliflower rice, add in the spinach and cilantro. Don't stir the leaves in, but just let them sit on top of the cauliflower rice. Cover the pan and let the leaves sit for about 2 to 3 minutes.

5.   Garnish the dish with sunflower seeds and ricotta cheese. Serve.

Did you know?
Cauliflowers can be eaten raw, cooked or pickled

Broccoli And Cheese Fritter

INGREDIENTS	Fats	Proteins	Carbs
1 cup broccoli, chopped	0.2 g	1.27 g	1.14 g
1/8 cup almond flour	6.19 g	2.62 g	2.67 g
1/2 cup mozzarella cheese	0 g	17.91 g	1.98 g
1 egg	9.64 g	8.97 g	1.02 g
0.5 tbsp. flaxseed meal	1.48 g	0.64 g	1.01 g
0.5 tsp. baking powder	0.01 g	0 g	1.17 g
3 tbsp. mayonnaise	14.31 g	2.68 g	1.38 g
1 tbsp. lemon juice	0.04 g	0.05 g	1.06 g
1 tbsp. fresh dill	0.09 g	0.28 g	0.56 g
4 tbsp coconut oil	54.4 g	0 g	0 g

Nutrition Facts

Amount per 212 g
1 serving (7.5 oz)

Calories 431
From fat 329

Amount	% Daily Value*	Amount	% Daily Value*
Total Fat 38g	58%	Total Carbohydrates 13g	4%
Saturated 16.6g	83%	Dietary Fiber 4g	14%
Trans Fat		Sugars 7g	
Cholesterol 84mg	28%	Protein 13g	26%
Sodium 96mg	4%		
Calcium 32% • Iron 12%		Vitamin A 27% • Vitamin C 17%	

* Percent Daily Values are based on 2000 calorie diet. Your Daily Values may be higher or lower depending on your calorie needs.

Directions

1.   Cut up the broccoli into florets and place inside a food processor. Pulse until the broccoli has been cut down to very small pieces.

2.   To the broccoli, add the almond flour, mozzarella cheese, 1 tbsp. flaxseed meal, and baking powder. You may also add salt and pepper at this point, if desired. Mix thoroughly.

3.   Add the egg to the mixture and mix thoroughly until everything is well-incorporated.

4.   Using your hands, form the mixture into balls of around 1 inch in diameter.

5.   Roll the balls around the remaining flaxseed meal, ensuring that they are completely covered. Continue doing this for all the balls and set them aside.

6.   Prepare the deep fryer. Add enough coconut oil to the deep fryer to fully submerge the balls you have made. Heat the deep fryer to about 375 F.

7.   Drop the balls one by one to the deep fryer, making sure that they don't stick to each other. Allow them to cook until golden brown, which should only take about 3 to 5 minutes.

8. Once they are cooked, drain the excess oil by placing the fritters on dish lined with paper towels.

9. To make a dip for the fritters, combine mayonnaise, dill, and lemon juice.

10. Serve the fritters with a side of dip. Enjoy!

Did you know?

Broccoli contains the flavonoid kaempferol. Kaempferol is an anti-inflammatory, helps fight against cancer and heart disease, and has been shown to be preventative in adult diabetes onset.

DAY 3

Meal	Recipe	Calories
Breakfast	Keto Smoothie Bowl	431
Lunch	Zucchini Grilled Cheese Sandwich	936
Dinner	Tofu and Bok Choy Salad	426

Keto Smoothie Bowl

INGREDIENTS	Fats	Proteins	Carbs
1/2 cup whole milk	1.04 g	1 g	1.52 g
1/2 cup cream	23.17 g	3.24 g	4.39 g
1/4 cup avocado, chopped	5.5 g	0.75 g	3.2 g
1/2 scoop protein powder	1.5 g	6.25 g	2.75 g
2 ice cubes	-	-	-
1/8 cup walnuts, chopped	6.78 g	1.58 g	1.43 g

Nutrition Facts

Amount per 212 g
1 serving (7.5 oz)

Calories 431
From fat 329

Amount	% Daily Value*	Amount	% Daily Value*
Total Fat 38g	58%	Total Carbohydrates 13g	4%
Saturated 16.6g	83%	Dietary Fiber 4g	14%
Trans Fat		Sugars 7g	
Cholesterol 84mg	28%	Protein 13g	26%
Sodium 96mg	4%		
Calcium 32% • Iron 12%		Vitamin A 27% • Vitamin C 17%	

* Percent Daily Values are based on 2000 calorie diet. Your Daily Values may be higher or lower depending on your calorie needs.

Directions

1. Place all the ingredients into a blender.

2. Blend until smooth.

3. Pour into a bowl.

4. Top with chopped walnuts and serve.

Did you know?

Walnuts are the oldest known tree food — they date back to 10,000 BC

Zucchini Grilled Cheese Sandwich

INGREDIENTS	Fats	Proteins	Carbs
2 cups zucchini, shredded	0.04 g	0.3 g	0.34 g
1 egg	9.64 g	8.97 g	1.02 g
1/8 cup parmesan cheese, shredded	3.62 g	3.69 g	1.81 g
1/2 cup cheddar, shredded	22.32 g	15.87 g	0.88 g
1/4tbsp. cornstarch	0 g	0.01 g	1.83 g
1/4 cup green onions, sliced	0.08 g	0.17 g	1.02 g
4 tbsp. coconut oil	54.4 g	0 g	0 g

Directions

1.　　Wrap the shredded zucchini in several pieces of kitchen towels. Place a weight (such as a pot with water) on top of the zucchini and allow it to squeeze the excess moisture out of it for at least an hour.

2.　　After enough water has been squeezed out of the zucchini shred, combine it with the egg, parmesan cheese, cornstarch, and green onions. Season with salt and pepper. Mix thoroughly.

3.　　In a large pan, pour enough coconut oil to coat the bottom of the pan. Heat the pan over medium heat.

4.　　When the pan is sufficiently hot, place about 1/4 cup of the zucchini mixture on the pan. Shape the zucchini mixture into a square.

5.　　Cook until golden brown on both sides. At this point, the fried mixture should resemble patties and should hold their shape.

6.　　Repeat until all of the zucchini mixture has been cooked. Drain excess oil from all cooked patties using paper towels.

7.　　To the same pan, place two zucchini patties. Top each patty with shredded cheddar and add another patty to each. Allow to cook until the cheese has melted.

8. Repeat until all zucchini patties have been made into sandwiches. Serve while hot.

Did you know?
The word zucchini comes from 'zucca' the Italian word for squash.

Tofu and Bok Choy Salad

INGREDIENTS	Fats	Proteins	Carbs
1/2 cup soft tofu, cubed	4.58 g	8.12 g	2.23 g
1/2 tsp. soy sauce	0.01 g	0.21 g	0.13 g
1 1/2 tsp. sesame oil	6.8 g	0 g	0 g
1 tsp. garlic, chopped	0.01 g	0.18 g	0.93 g
1 tsp. lemon juice	0.01 g	0.02 g	0.35 g
3/4 cups bok choy, cooked	0.2 g	1.98 g	2.26 g
1/2 cup cilantro, chopped	0.04 g	0.17 g	0.29 g
1/4 cup green onions, chopped	0.08 g	0.17 g	1.02 g
2 tbsp. coconut oil	27.2 g	0 g	0 g
1/4 tbsp. soy sauce	0.01 g	0.33 g	0.2 g
1/4 tbsp. peanut butter	1.53 g	1.17 g	1.6 g
1/2 tbsp. lime juice	0.01 g	0.03 g	0.64 g

Nutrition Facts

Amount per 337 g
1 serving (11.9 oz)

Calories 426
From fat 349

Amount	% Daily Value*	Amount	% Daily Value*
Total Fat 40.5g	62%	Total Carbohydrates 10g	3%
Saturated 25.5g	127%	Dietary Fiber 2g	10%
Trans Fat 0g		Sugars 3g	
Cholesterol 0mg	0%	Protein 12g	25%
Sodium 574mg	24%		
Calcium 28% • Iron 18%		Vitamin A 133% • Vitamin C 72%	

* Percent Daily Values are based on 2000 calorie diet. Your Daily Values may be higher or lower depending on your calorie needs.

Directions

1.   In a large container, mix the cubed tofu with the soy sauce, sesame oil, garlic, and lemon juice. Season with salt and pepper. Marinate the tofu in the mixture for at least an hour.

2.   After marinating, pre-heat your oven to 350 F.

3.   Place the tofu cubes on a large baking tray lines with parchment paper. Make sure that the cubes are not in contact with one another to ensure even cooking.

4.   Bake the tofu for 30 to 35 minutes. They should come out golden brown and have a crispy exterior.

5.   In a separate bowl, mix the coconut oil, soy sauce, peanut butter, and lime juice. Mix thoroughly until well-incorporated.

6.   To this bowl, add the chopped cilantro and spring onions. Mix well.

7.   Chop the bok choy into bite-sized strips.

8.   Just before serving, add the dressing to the chopped bok choy.

9.   Once the tofu is cooked, mix the tofu cubes with the bok choy salad.

10.   Serve immediately and enjoy!

Did you know?

Tofu contains all 8 essential amino acids. It is rich in magnesium, phosphorus and selenium too (which helps to trigger happy hormones). Tofu also contains copper, vitamin B1, calcium and iron. It is low in fat but high on nutrition. Research shows that regular tofu eaters get enhanced protection against different kinds of cancer and heart diseases too.

DAY 4

Meal	Recipe	Calories
Breakfast	Feta Cheese Salad with Balsamic Butter	711
Lunch	Mexican Cauliflower Rice	346
Dinner	Pumpkin and Spinach Cannelloni	879

Feta Cheese Salad with Balsamic Butter

INGREDIENTS	Fats	Proteins	Carbs
1/2 cup feta cheese, crumbled	15.96 g	10.66 g	3.07 g
1/8 cup pumpkin seeds	7.5 g	4.57 g	2.25 g
1/4 cup butter	46.07 g	0.48 g	0.03 g
1 tbsp. balsamic vinegar	0 g	0.08 g	2.72 g
1/2 cup baby spinach	0.06 g	0.43 g	0.54 g

Nutrition Facts

Amount per 178 g
1 serving (6.3 oz)

Calories 711
From fat 609

	Amount	% Daily Value*	Amount	% Daily Value*
	Total Fat 69.6g	107%	Total Carbohydrates 9g	3%
	Saturated 41.7g	209%	Dietary Fiber 1g	5%
	Trans Fat 1.9g		Sugars 6g	
	Cholesterol 189mg	63%	Protein 16g	32%
	Sodium 1108mg	46%		
	Calcium 41% • Iron 13%		Vitamin A 63% • Vitamin C 8%	

* Percent Daily Values are based on 2000 calorie diet. Your Daily Values may be higher or lower depending on your calorie needs.

Directions

1.   Preheat the oven to 400 °F.

2.   Spread the crumbled feta cheese on a greased baking tray and bake in the oven for 10 minutes.

3.   In a dry frying pan over high heat, toast the pumpkin seeds until they start to pop.

4.   Lower the heat. Add the butter and let simmer until the butter has developed a golden brown color.

5.   Add balsamic vinegar and let simmer for 1 to 2 minutes. Turn off the heat.

6.   Assemble the baby spinach leaves on a dish. Pour the balsamic butter on the baby spinach and top with the feta cheese.

Did you know?

Balsamic vinegar has minerals that prevents bone diseases such as osteoporosis, prevent strokes, treat anemia and fatigue, as well as lower high blood pressure and high cholesterol

Mexican Cauliflower Rice

INGREDIENTS	Fats	Proteins	Carbs
1/2 cup cauliflower, chopped	0.15 g	1.03 g	2.66 g
2 tbsp. olive oil	27 g	0 g	0 g
1 tbsp. onion, chopped	0.01 g	0.11 g	0.93 g
1/2 tbsp. garlic, chopped	0.02 g	0.27 g	1.42 g
1 tbsp jalapeno	0.03 g	0.07 g	0.52 g

1/4 cup tomatoes, chopped	0.07 g	0.33 g	1.45 g
1/4 cup bell peppers, chopped	0.02 g	0.23 g	1.07 g
1 tsp. cumin powder	0.47 g	0.37 g	0.93 g
1/2 tsp. paprika	0.15 g	0.17 g	0.65 g
1/4 cup avocado, sliced	5.35 g	0.73 g	3.11 g

Nutrition Facts

Amount per 191 g
1 serving (6.7 oz)

Calories 346
From fat 291

Amount	% Daily Value*	Amount	% Daily Value*
Total Fat 33.3g	51%	Total Carbohydrates 13g	4%
Saturated 4.7g	23%	Dietary Fiber 5g	21%
Trans Fat 0g		Sugars 4g	
Cholesterol 0mg	0%	Protein 3g	7%
Sodium 28mg	1%		
Calcium 6% • Iron 14%		Vitamin A 24% • Vitamin C 123%	

* Percent Daily Values are based on 2000 calorie diet. Your Daily Values may be higher or lower depending on your calorie needs.

Directions:

1. Add the chopped cauliflower to a good processor. Pulse until cauliflower has been chopped to small bits, with texture resembling rice.

2. Heat the olive oil in a pan over medium heat. Add the onions, garlic, and jalapeno. Stir fry until fragrant.

3. Add the tomatoes, paprika, and cumin powder to the pan. Cook until the tomatoes have softened.

4.   Add the bell peppers and cauliflower tice to the pan. Stir fry until the cauliflower rice is tender which should take about 3 to 4 minutes. Season with salt and pepper, as desired.

5.   Top with the sliced avocado and serve.

Did you know?

Compared to green peppers, red peppers are known to have more vitamins and nutrients and contain the antioxidant lycopene. The level of carotene, like lycopene, is nine times higher in red peppers. Red peppers have twice the vitamin C content of green peppers.

Pumpkin and Spinach Cannelloni

INGREDIENTS	Fats	Proteins	Carbs
1/4 cup pumpkin, cubed	0.03 g	0.29 g	1.89 g
3 slices onion leeks	0.05 g	0.27 g	2.55 g
1/4 cup cauliflower, chopped	0.08 g	0.51 g	1.33 g
1 tsp. fresh thyme	0.01 g	0.04 g	0.2 g
2 tbsp. olive oil	27 g	0 g	0 g

3 tbsp. goat's cheese	8.54 g	7.32 g	0.52 g
1/2 cup spinach	0.06 g	0.43 g	0.54 g
1/4 cup cream cheese	17.16 g	4.26 g	2.1 g
1/4 cup heavy whipping cream	11.1 g	0.62 g	0.84 g
1 tbsp. fresh basil	0.02 g	0.09 g	0.07 g
1 tbsp. parmesan cheese, grated	1.39 g	1.42 g	0.7 g
1 egg	4.18 g	5.53 g	0.32 g
1/4 cup cheddar cheese	11.16 g	7.93 g	0.44 g
1/4 tbsp. garlic	0.01 g	0.13 g	0.69 g

Directions:

1.   Preheat the oven to 360 °F.

2.   Place the pumpkin and cauliflower on a baking tray. Sprinkle the thyme over the vegetables and drizzle with olive oil. Bake the vegetables for 35 to 45 minutes until they are soft and caramelized.

3.   Remove from the oven and let cool.

4.   When the vegetables have cooled down, mash them with a fork or potato ricer.

5.   To the mashed vegetables, add the goat's cheese and spinach.

6.   Separate the layers of the sliced leeks. We will only be using the outermost layers in this recipe.

7.   Cook the separated layers in boiling water for 2 to 3 minutes. The goal is to make them slightly tender without being soggy. Once they are soft, remove them from the pot and place in cold water.

8.   Combine the cream cheese and heavy whipping cream. Mix until smooth.

9.   To the cream cheese mixture, add the basil, parmesan cheese, garlic, and eggs. Mix until thoroughly combined.

10.   Spread a layer of the cheese mixture on the bottom of the lasagna dish.

11.   In each layer of the leeks, place about three tablespoons of the mashed vegetable mixture. Roll the leek around the filling, ensuring that the filling is well distributed. Place the finished roll on top of the cheese mixture on the lasagna dish.

12.   Repeat previous step until all leek layers or all the mashed vegetable mixture has been consumed.

13.   Pour the remained of the cheese mixture on top of the rolled leeks.

14.   Sprinkle grated cheddar and parmesan cheese over the top.

15.   Bake the dish at 360 °F for about 30 minutes, or until the top has browned.

16.   Remove the dish from the oven and let cool before serving.

Did you know?
Each pumpkin has about 500 seeds.

DAY 5

Meal	Recipe	Calories
Breakfast	Spinach Artichoke Breakfast Casserole	462
Lunch	Spaghetti Squash with Creamy Mushroom Sauce	919
Dinner	Cauliflower Macaroni and Cheese	597

Spinach Artichoke Breakfast Casserole

INGREDIENTS	Fats	Proteins	Carbs
1 egg	4.18 g	5.53 g	0.32 g
1/8 cup whole milk	1.04 g	1 g	1.52 g
1/4 cup spinach	0.03 g	0.21 g	0.27 g
1/4 cup artichoke hearts	0.04 g	0.78 g	2.52 g
1/4 tbsp. garlic, chopped	0.01 g	0.13 g	0.69 g
1 tbsp. coconut flour	0.03 g	0.11 g	0.56 g

1/2 tsp. baking powder	0.01 g	0 g	1.17 g
1 tbsp. olive oil	13.5 g	0 g	0 g
1/4 cup feta cheese, crumbled	7.98 g	5.33 g	1.53 g
2 tbsp. unsalted butter	15.43 g	0.92 g	0 g

Nutrition Facts

Amount per 206 g
1 serving (7.3 oz)

Calories 462
From fat 376

Amount	% Daily Value*	Amount	% Daily Value*
Total Fat 42.2g	65%	Total Carbohydrates 9g	3%
Saturated 19.1g	95%	Dietary Fiber 2g	7%
Trans Fat 0g		Sugars 4g	
Cholesterol 230mg	77%	Protein 14g	28%
Sodium 477mg	20%		
Calcium 39% • Iron 12%		Vitamin A 33% • Vitamin C 10%	

* Percent Daily Values are based on a 2000 calorie diet. Your Daily Values may be higher or lower depending on your calorie needs

Directions:

1.   Grease the inside of a deep pan with olive oil. Heat the pan under medium heat.

2.   In a large bowl, whisk together the eggs, milk, spinach, artichoke hearts, feta cheese, butter, and garlic. Season with salt and pepper, if desired. Mix until thoroughly combined.

3.   Add the coconut flour and baking powder to the egg mixture and mix until well combined.

4.   Spread the mixture into the deep pan. Cover and allow to cook for about 7 to 10 minutes, or until the top layer has set.

5. Allow to cool and serve.

Did you know?
The artichoke is technically a flower bud that has not yet bloomed.

Spaghetti Squash with Creamy Mushroom Sauce

INGREDIENTS	Fats	Proteins	Carbs
1/2 cup spaghetti squash	0.29 g	0.32 g	3.49 g
2 tbsp. olive oil	27 g	0 g	0 g
1/4 cup white mushrooms, sliced	0.06 g	0.54 g	0.57 g
1 tbsp. onions, sliced	0.01 g	0.11 g	0.93 g
1/4 cup butter	46.07 g	0.48 g	0.03 g
1 tsp. Dijon mustard	0.17 g	0.19 g	0.29 g
1 tbsp. sage	0.26 g	0.21 g	1.21 g

1 tsp. thyme	0.01 g	0.04 g	0.2 g
1/4 cup spinach	0.03 g	0.21 g	0.27 g
1/4 cup cheddar, diced	11.16 g	7.93 g	0.44 g
1/4 cup heavy whipping cream	11.1 g	0.62 g	0.84 g

Nutrition Facts

Amount per 240 g
1 serving (8.5 oz)

Calories 919
From fat 849

Amount	% Daily Value*	Amount	% Daily Value*
Total Fat 96.2g	148%	Total Carbohydrates 8g	3%
Saturated 46.4g	232%	Dietary Fiber 2g	10%
Trans Fat 2.3g		Sugars 3g	
Cholesterol 197mg	66%	Protein 11g	21%
Sodium 661mg	28%		
Calcium 32% • Iron 8%		Vitamin A 62% • Vitamin C 11%	

* Percent Daily Values are based on 2000 calorie diet. Your Daily Values may be higher or lower depending on your calorie needs.

Directions:

1. Preheat the oven to 375 F.

2. Place the spaghetti squash on a medium-sized baking tray. Drizzle with olive oil and season with salt and pepper.

3. Bake the squash for about 60 minutes, or until the flash has been softened enough to be easily pierced with a knife.

4. Melt the butter in a frying pan over medium heat.

5.   Cook the mushrooms in the butter until they are golden brown.

6.   Add the onions and cook until they are translucent and fragrant.

7.   In a small mixing bowl, combine the Dijon mustard, sage, thyme, cheddar, and heavy whipping cream. Add 2 tbsp. of water and whisk until thoroughly combined.

8.   Add the mixture from step 7 to the cooked mushrooms and onions. Turn the heat down to low and stir until well combined.

9.   Add in the spinach and let the leaves wilt for 1 to 2 minutes.

10.   Remove the cooked squash from the oven and scrape the flesh off to form spaghetti-like strands.

11.   In a bowl, pour the mushroom sauce over the spaghetti squash. Serve and enjoy.

Did you know?

Mushrooms are a fungus, and unlike plants, mushrooms do not require sunlight to make energy for themselves.

Cauliflower Macaroni and Cheese

INGREDIENTS	Fats	Proteins	Carbs
1/2 cup cauliflower, chopped	0.15 g	1.03 g	2.66 g
1/4 cup coconut milk	12.05 g	1.14 g	1.59 g
1 tbsp. desiccated coconut	5.16 g	0.55 g	1.89 g

1 egg	0.06 g	3.6 g	0.24 g
3/4 cup cheddar cheese, diced	33.48 g	23.8 g	1.32 g

Nutrition Facts	Amount	% Daily Value*	Amount	% Daily Value*
Amount per 250 g	Total Fat 50.9g	78%	Total Carbohydrates 8g	3%
1 serving (8.8 oz)	Saturated 34.5g	173%	Dietary Fiber 2g	10%
	Trans Fat 1.2g		Sugars 2g	
Calories 597	Cholesterol 101mg	34%	Protein 30g	60%
From fat 447	Sodium 719mg	30%		
	Calcium 70% • Iron 14%		Vitamin A 20% • Vitamin C 44%	
	* Percent Daily Values are based on 2000 calorie diet. Your Daily Values may be higher or lower depending on your calorie needs.			

Directions:

1.   Cook the chopped cauliflower in a steamer until al dente.

2.   In a large skillet, heat up the coconut milk over medium heat. Add the desiccated coconut and allow the mixture to bubble.

3.   Take the coconut mixture off the heat and whisk in the egg. Allow the sauce to thicken.

4.   Spread the cooked cauliflower in a deep baking dish. Pour in the coconut sauce and sprinkle the cheese evenly on the top.

5. Bake in the oven at 350 °F for 35 to 40 minutes. Broil the top for 3 to 5 minutes to get a brown and crunchy finish.

Did you know?
Cauliflower can grow from 8 to 30 inches both in height and width.

DAY 6

Meal	Recipe	Calories
Breakfast	Keto Yogurt Bowl	330
Lunch	Lettuce and Walnut Salad	774
Dinner	Avocado Walnut Pesto	712

Keto Yogurt Bowl

INGREDIENTS	Fats	Proteins	Carbs
1/2 cup Greek yogurt	0.47 g	12.23 g	4.32 g

2 tbsp. desiccated coconut	11.05 g	0.85 g	3.44 g
1 tbsp. sunflower seeds	4.53 g	1.83 g	1.76 g
1 tbsp. almond butter	8.88 g	3.35 g	3.01 g

Nutrition Facts

Amount per 161 g
1 serving (5.7 oz)

Calories 330
From fat 209

Amount	% Daily Value*	Amount	% Daily Value*
Total Fat 24.9g	38%	Total Carbohydrates 13g	4%
Saturated 11g	55%	Dietary Fiber 2g	10%
Trans Fat 0g		Sugars 5g	
Cholesterol 6mg	2%	Protein 18g	37%
Sodium 51mg	2%		
Calcium 20% • Iron 9%		Vitamin A 0% • Vitamin C 1%	

* Percent Daily Values are based on 2000 calorie diet. Your Daily Values may be higher or lower depending on your calorie needs.

Directions:

1.   In a medium-sized bowl, add the Greek yogurt and drizzle with almond butter.

2.   Top with the desiccated coconut and sunflower seeds. Serve and enjoy.

Did you know?

There two types of sunflower seeds: black and striped Black sunflower seeds are used to make oil and snacks are made out of striped seeds.

Lettuce and Walnut Salad

INGREDIENTS	Fats	Proteins	Carbs
1 tbsp. light sour cream	1.27 g	0.42 g	0.85 g
1 tbsp. mayonnaise	10.33 g	0.13 g	0.08 g
1 tsp. parsley	0.01 g	0.04 g	0.08 g
1 tbsp. milk	0.49 g	0.47 g	0.72 g
1 egg, boiled	4.18 g	5.53 g	0.32 g
1/2 cup cheddar, diced	22.32 g	15.87 g	0.88 g
3/4 cup romaine lettuce	0.11 g	0.43 g	1.16 g
1/4 cup cucumber, cubed	0.05 g	0.18 g	0.64 g
1 tsp. Dijon mustard	0.17 g	0.19 g	0.29 g
1/4 cup walnuts, chopped	19.11 g	4.46 g	4.02 g
1 tbsp. olive oil	13.5 g	0 g	0 g

Nutrition Facts

Amount per 265 g
1 serving (9.3 oz)

Calories 774
From fat 630

Amount	% Daily Value*	Amount	% Daily Value*
Total Fat 71.5g	110%	Total Carbohydrates 9g	3%
Saturated 20.5g	103%	Dietary Fiber 3g	13%
Trans Fat 0.8g		Sugars 3g	
Cholesterol 242mg	81%	Protein 28g	55%
Sodium 652mg	27%		
Calcium 56% • Iron 13%		Vitamin A 84% • Vitamin C 8%	

* Percent Daily Values are based on 2000 calorie diet. Your Daily Values may be higher or lower depending on your calorie needs.

Directions:

1. In a dry frying pan over medium heat, lightly toast the chopped walnuts for about 2 to 3 minutes.

2. Prepare the dressing by mixing together the sour cream, mayonnaise, parsley, Dijon mustard, olive oil, and milk. Whisk together until thoroughly combined.

3. Assemble the salad. Toss together the romaine lettuce, cheddar, slices of the boiled egg, and the toasted walnuts.

4. Mix in the dressing and toss. Serve.

Did you know?

Lettuce provides dietary fibers, vitamins A, B9 and C and minerals such as calcium, iron and copper. Darker varieties provide more nutrients than light green varieties.

Avocado Walnut Pesto

INGREDIENTS	Fats	Proteins	Carbs
1 medium zucchini	0.04 g	0.3 g	0.34 g
1/4 cup avocado, cubed	5.5 g	0.75 g	3.2 g
1 tbsp. basil, chopped	0.02 g	0.09 g	0.07 g
1 tbsp. walnuts, chopped	4.63 g	1.88 g	0.75 g
1 tbsp. garlic, chopped	0.02 g	0.27 g	1.42 g
1 tbsp. lemon juice	0.04 g	0.05 g	1.06 g
1 tbsp. parmesan, grated	1.39 g	1.42 g	0.7 g
2 tbsp. olive oil	27 g	0 g	0 g
1/2 cup cheddar cheese, grated	19.11 g	13.58 g	0.75 g
1 tbsp. butter	11.52 g	0.12 g	0.01 g

Nutrition Facts

Amount per 181 g
1 serving (6.4 oz)

Calories 712
From fat 610

Amount	% Daily Value*	Amount	% Daily Value*
Total Fat 69.3g	107%	Total Carbohydrates 8g	3%
Saturated 23.8g	119%	Dietary Fiber 3g	13%
Trans Fat 1.2g		Sugars 1g	
Cholesterol 92mg	31%	Protein 18g	37%
Sodium 460mg	19%		
Calcium 45% • Iron 5%		Vitamin A 24% • Vitamin C 26%	

* Percent Daily Values are based on 2000 calorie diet. Your Daily Values may be higher or lower depending on your calorie needs.

Directions:

1.   Cut the zucchini into thin ribbons using a mandolin slicer.

2.   Place the zucchini ribbons in a bowl and sprinkle with some salt. Set aside.

3.   In a food processor, combine the olive oil, butter, parmesan cheese, lemon juice, walnuts, avocado, and garlic.

4.   Pulse the food processor until the pesto sauce is smooth and consistent.

5.   Heat some olive oil in a saucepan and sauté the zucchini ribbons just until they start to soften. Remove from heat.

6.   Mix the pesto sauce and zucchini ribbons. Toss until all the zucchini ribbons have been coated.

7.   Top with grated cheddar cheese before serving.

Did you know?

Avocados are one of the only fruits that contain heart-healthy monounsaturated fat (the good-for-you fat) that helps boost good (HDL) cholesterol and lowers bad (LDL) cholesterol

DAY 7

Meal	Recipe	Calories
Breakfast	Brie and Pecan Crepes	738
Lunch	Broccoli and Cheese Soup	509
Dinner	Crunchy Cauliflower and Pine Nut Salad	638

Brie and Pecan Crepes

INGREDIENTS	Fats	Proteins	Carbs
1/2 cup cream cheese	34.32 g	8.52 g	4.2 g
1 egg	4.18 g	5.53 g	0.32 g
1/8 tsp baking soda	0 g	0 g	0 g
1/4 cup pecans, halved	17.85 g	2.27 g	3.44 g
1/4 cup butter	2.92 g	0.03 g	0 g

1/2 tsp. cinnamon powder	0.02 g	0.05 g	1.05 g
1/4 cup brie, diced	9.96 g	7.47 g	0.16 g

Nutrition Facts

Amount per 230 g
1 serving (8.1 oz)

Calories 738
From fat 609

Amount	% Daily Value*	Amount	% Daily Value*
Total Fat 69.3g	107%	Total Carbohydrates 9g	3%
Saturated 32.7g	163%	Dietary Fiber 3g	12%
Trans Fat 0.1g		Sugars 6g	
Cholesterol 315mg	105%	Protein 24g	48%
Sodium 1000mg	42%		
Calcium 21% • Iron 17%		Vitamin A 36% • Vitamin C 1%	

* Percent Daily Values are based on 2000 calorie diet. Your Daily Values may be higher or lower depending on your calorie needs.

Directions:

1.   In a large bowl, combine the ingredients for the batter mix: cream cheese, egg, baking, soda, and salt. Whisk together until smooth.

2.   In a small non-stick pan, melt half of the butter over medium heat.

3.   Ladle the crepe batter into the pan and swirl the pan so that the better is spread thinly and evenly. Let one side cook until the top looks dry and flip gently. Cook the other side only for a few seconds.

4.   Repeat the previous steps until all the batter mix has been consumed.

5.   Melt the remaining butter in a small pan over medium heat and toast the chopped pecans until fragrant. Be careful not to burn them.

6.   Sprinkle the cinnamon powder over the toasted pecans and mix. Set aside to cool.

7.   Assemble the sliced brie cheese on the crepe and top with toasted pecans. Fold or roll up the crepes.

8.   Repeat until all the toppings or crepes have been used. Serve.

Did you know?
The name "pecan" is a Native American word that was used to describe nuts requiring a stone to crack.

Broccoli and Cheese Soup

INGREDIENTS	Fats	Proteins	Carbs
3/4 cup broccoli, chopped	0.15 g	0.95 g	0.86 g
1/2 cup vegetable broth	1.02 g	2.13 g	7.3 g
1/4 cup cheddar, diced	11.16 g	7.93 g	0.44 g

1/4 cup heavy whipping cream	11.1 g	0.62 g	0.84 g
1/8 cup butter	23.9 3 g	0.25 g	0.02 g
1/4 tsp. mustard powder	0.18 g	0.13 g	0.14 g
1/8 tsp. nutmeg	0.11 g	0.02 g	0.15 g
1/4 tsp. garlic powder	0.01 g	0.13 g	0.58 g
1/4 tsp. onion powder	0.01 g	0.06 g	0.47 g

Nutrition Facts

Amount per 242 g

1 serving (8.5 oz)

Calories 509

From fat 421

Amount	% Daily Value*	Amount	% Daily Value*
Total Fat 47.7g	73%	Total Carbohydrates 11g	4%
Saturated 28.8g	144%	Dietary Fiber 3g	10%
Trans Fat 1.4g		Sugars 3g	
Cholesterol 138mg	46%	Protein 12g	24%
Sodium 708mg	30%		
Calcium 30% • Iron 8%		Vitamin A 65% • Vitamin C 24%	

* Percent Daily Values are based on 2000 calorie diet. Your Daily Values may be higher or lower depending on your calorie needs.

Directions:

1.   Cook the chopped broccoli in a steam for 4 to 5 minutes.

2.   In a blender, combine the cooked broccoli with all other ingredients. Blend until smooth.

3.   Transfer the contents of the blender into a small pot. Simmer the soup over medium heat for

about 10 minutes. Season with salt and pepper, if desired.

4.   Serve hot.

Did you know?

Broccoli is also very high in Vitamin A. Vitamin A helps fight cancer within your cells, as well as keep your eyes healthy and stave off glaucoma and other eye degenerative diseases. It also helps to promote healthy skin, break down urinary stones (a big issue with the summer heat and dehydration) and maintain healthy bones and teeth.

Crunchy Cauliflower and

Pine Nut Salad

INGREDIENTS	Fats	Proteins	Carbs
1/4 cup cauliflower, chopped	0.08 g	0.51 g	1.33 g
2 tbsp. onion leeks, chopped	0.03 g	0.17 g	1.57 g
1/4 cup pine nuts, chopped	11.55 g	2.31 g	2.21 g

2 tbsp. sour cream	2.54 g	0.84 g	1.7 g
1/2 cup iceberg lettuce, shredded	0.05 g	0.32 g	1.07 g
1/4 cup mayonnaise	41.17 g	0.53 g	0.31 g
1/4 cup feta cheese, crumbled	7.98 g	5.33 g	1.53 g

Nutrition Facts

Amount per 207 g
1 serving (7.3 oz)

Calories 638
From fat 562

	Amount	% Daily Value*	Amount	% Daily Value*
Total Fat	63.4g	98%	Total Carbohydrates 10g	3%
Saturated	14.5g	72%	Dietary Fiber 2g	7%
Trans Fat	0.1g		Sugars 4g	
Cholesterol	65mg	22%	Protein 10g	20%
Sodium	727mg	30%		
Calcium 25% • Iron 10%			Vitamin A 13% • Vitamin C 26%	

* Percent Daily Values are based on 2000 calorie diet. Your Daily Values may be higher or lower depending on your calorie needs.

Directions:

1.   In a small pan, toast the pine nut overs medium heat until fragrant.

2.   In a large bowl, combine all the ingredient including the toasted pine nuts.

3.   For best results, refrigerate the salad for at least 2 hours and serve cold.

Did you know?

Pine nuts are one of the calorie-rich edible nuts. 100 g of dry-kernels provide 673 calories. Additionally, they comprise of numerous health promoting phyto-chemicals, vitamins, antioxidants, and minerals.

DAY 8

Meal	Recipe	Calories
Breakfast	Keto Breakfast Muffin	480
Lunch	Thai Soup with Tofu	627
Dinner	Asparagus and Tofu Mash	601

Keto Breakfast Muffin

INGREDIENTS	Fats	Proteins	Carbs
1 egg	23.11 g	30.52 g	1.75 g
1/2 tsp. olive oil	2.3 g	0 g	0 g
1/4 cup spinach	0.03 g	0.21 g	0.27 g
1/4 cup white mushrooms, sliced	0.06 g	0.54 g	0.57 g
1 tbsp. green onion, sliced	0.03 g	0.06 g	0.34 g

1/4 cup parmesan cheese, grated	6.96 g	7.11 g	3.48 g

Nutrition Facts	Amount	% Daily Value*	Amount	% Daily Value*
	Total Fat 32.5g	50%	Total Carbohydrates 6g	2%
	Saturated 11.8g	59%	Dietary Fiber 0g	2%
Amount per 301 g	Trans Fat 0.3g		Sugars 2g	
1 serving (10.6 oz)	Cholesterol 925mg	308%	Protein 38g	77%
	Sodium 804mg	34%		
Calories 480				
From fat 291	Calcium 36% • Iron 26%		Vitamin A 50% • Vitamin C	6%

* Percent Daily Values are based on 2000 calorie diet. Your Daily Values may be higher or lower depending on your calorie needs.

Directions:

1. Preheat your oven to 350 F.

2. In a small bowl, crack the egg and whisk. Season with salt, if desired.

3. Apply olive oil to a muffin pan. In one portion of the pan, add the spinach, mushrooms, green onion, and cheese.

4. Pour the eggs over the contents of the muffin tin.

5. Bake for about 20 minutes, or until the top of the egg has set.

6. Remove from the oven and let the cooked muffin rest for a few minutes. Remove the muffin

from the tin using a rubber spatula or by inverting the muffin pan.

7.   Serve immediately.

Did you know?
Extra virgin olive oil comes from the first pressing of the olives with no chemicals used to extract the oil. This means it has a wonderful, fresh, clean taste

Thai Soup with Tofu

INGREDIENTS	Fats	Proteins	Carbs
1 tbsp. bell pepper, diced	0.01 g	0.07 g	0.27 g
1/4 tbsp. white mushrooms, sliced	0.06 g	0.54 g	0.57 g
1/4 tbsp. garlic, chopped	0.01 g	0.13 g	0.69 g
1/4 tbsp. ginger, sliced thinly	0.01 g	0.03 g	0.27 g
1/4 tbsp. chili powder	0.29 g	0.27 g	0.99 g
3/4 cup coconut milk	36.15 g	3.42 g	4.76 g
1/4 cup silky tofu, cubed	2.29 g	4.06 g	1.12 g
1/2 tbsp. soy sauce	0.02 g	0.64 g	0.4 g
1/2 tbsp. lime juice	0.01 g	0.03 g	0.64 g
1/4 tbsp. cilantro	0 g	0.01 g	0.02 g
2 tbsp. coconut oil	27.2 g	0 g	0 g

Nutrition Facts

Amount per 297 g
1 serving (10.5 oz)

Calories 627
From fat 560

Amount	% Daily Value*	Amount	% Daily Value*
Total Fat 66.1g	102%	Total Carbohydrates 10g	3%
Saturated 56g	280%	Dietary Fiber 1g	5%
Trans Fat 0g		Sugars 1g	
Cholesterol 0mg	0%	Protein 9g	18%
Sodium 342mg	14%		
Calcium 12% • Iron 38%		Vitamin A 13% • Vitamin C 22%	

* Percent Daily Values are based on 2000 calorie diet. Your Daily Values may be higher or lower depending on your calorie needs.

Directions:

1.   In a medium-sized pot, combine the coconut milk, onion, bell pepper, mushrooms, garlic, ginger, and chili powder.

2.   Bring the coconut mixture to a boil and cook over medium heat for 5 to 7 minutes.

3.   Add the diced tofu to the pot. Mix and cook for another additional 5 minutes.

4.   Remove the pot from heat. Add the soy sauce and lime juice. Stir in the new ingredients.

5.   To serve, scoop the soup onto a bowl and top with fresh cilantro.

Did you know?
When picking out garlic at the grocery store, choose firm, tight, heavy, dry bulbs.

Asparagus and Tofu Mash

INGREDIENTS	Fats	Proteins	Carbs
1/2 cup asparagus, chopped	0.08 g	1.47 g	2.6 g
1 tbsp. spring onion, chopped	0.01 g	0.11 g	0.44 g
4 tbsp. coconut cream	20.81 g	2.18 g	3.99 g
1/2 tbsp. parsley	0.02 g	0.06 g	0.12 g
1 tsp. lemon juice	0.01 g	0.02 g	0.35 g
2 tbsp. coconut oil	27.2 g	0 g	0 g
1 cup silky tofu. cubed	9.15 g	16.24 g	4.46 g

Nutrition Facts

Amount per 415 g
1 serving (14.6 oz)

Calories 601
From fat 486

	Amount	% Daily Value*	Amount	% Daily Value*
	Total Fat 57.3g	88%	Total Carbohydrates 12g	4%
	Saturated 43.3g	217%	Dietary Fiber 4g	14%
	Trans Fat 0g		Sugars 3g	
	Cholesterol 0mg	0%	Protein 20g	40%
	Sodium 26mg	1%		
	Calcium 31% • Iron 32%		Vitamin A 15% • Vitamin C 19%	

* Percent Daily Values are based on 2000 calorie diet. Your Daily Values may be higher or lower depending on your calorie needs.

Directions:

1.   Cook the tofu cubes in a steamer for 8 to 10 minutes.

2.   In a pot of boiling water, blanch the chopped asparagus for 2 minutes. Drain immediately.

3.   In a small pan over medium heat, sauté the spring onions in coconut oil.

4.   In a blender, mix together the tofu, asparagus, spring onions, coconut cream, lemon juice, and parsley. Season with salt and pepper, if desired.

5.   Blend the mixture until smooth

6.   Serve while hot.

Did you know?
Asparagus contains NO fat or cholesterol.

DAY 9

Meal	Recipe	Calories
Breakfast	Mediterranean Vegetable Frittata	762
Lunch	Keto Cheese Pizza	553
Dinner	Keto Pasta with Blue Cheese Sauce	749

Mediterranean Vegetable Frittata

INGREDIENTS	Fats	Proteins	Carbs
2 eggs	8.37 g	11.05 g	0.63 g
2 tbsp. butter	23.04 g	0.24 g	0.02 g
1/4 cup heavy cream	11.1 g	0.62 g	0.84 g
1/2 cup cheddar, diced	22.32 g	15.87 g	0.88 g
1 cup spinach	0.12 g	0.86 g	1.09 g
1 tbsp. olives, sliced	0.9 g	0.07 g	0.53 g

1/2 tbsp. garlic, chopped	0.02 g	0.27 g	1.42 g
1/4 cup bell pepper, chopped	3.41 g	0.22 g	1.22 g
1 tbsp. parsley	0.03 g	0.11 g	0.24 g

Nutrition Facts

Amount per 288 g
1 serving (10.1 oz)

Calories 762
From fat 616

Amount	% Daily Value*	Amount	% Daily Value*
Total Fat 69.3g	107%	Total Carbohydrates 7g	2%
Saturated 37.6g	188%	Dietary Fiber 2g	7%
Trans Fat 1.7g		Sugars 2g	
Cholesterol 497mg	166%	Protein 29g	59%
Sodium 837mg	35%		
Calcium 57% • Iron 18%		Vitamin A 111% • Vitamin C 110%	

* Percent Daily Values are based on 2000 calorie diet. Your Daily Values may be higher or lower depending on your calorie needs.

Directions:

1.   Preheat the oven to 350 F.

2.   Coat the bottom and side of a spring form pan with the softened butter.

3.   In a small frying pan, melt a small pat of butter under medium heat.

4.   To the frying pan, add the garlic, olives, and bell pepper. Saute for 2 to 3 minutes until the pepper has softened.

5.   Add the spinach and stir until wilted.

6.   In a large bowl, whisk together the eggs and heavy cream until thoroughly mixed and airy.

7.   Pour the whisked egg on the springform pan.

8.   Drop in the cooked vegetables, spreading them as evenly as possible.

9.   Add diced cheddar to the top.

10.   Bake in the oven for 25 to 30 minutes, or until the top has developed a golden brown color.

11.   Let cool and serve with a garnish of parsley.

Did you know?

Parsley was used in the ancient Rome as ingredient of salads, to eliminate effects of hangover and as ornament in the form of garlands for the head.

Keto Cheese Pizza

INGREDIENTS	Fats	Proteins	Carbs
3/4 cup cauliflower, chopped	0.22 g	1.54 g	3.99 g
1 egg	4.18 g	5.53 g	0.32 g
1 tbsp. coconut flour	5.53 g	0.42 g	1.72 g
1 tbsp. avocado oil	14 g	0 g	0 g
1 tbsp. tomato puree	0.03 g	0.26 g	1.4 g
1 cup mozzarella, shredded	25.03 g	24.83 g	2.45 g

Nutrition Facts

Amount per 274 g
1 serving (9.7 oz)

Calories 603
From fat 430

Amount	% Daily Value*	Amount	% Daily Value*
Total Fat 49g	75%	Total Carbohydrates 10g	3%
Saturated 22.7g	114%	Dietary Fiber 2g	8%
Trans Fat 0g		Sugars 4g	
Cholesterol 252mg	84%	Protein 33g	65%
Sodium 796mg	33%		
Calcium 61% • Iron 12%		Vitamin A 21% • Vitamin C 68%	

* Percent Daily Values are based on 2000 calorie diet. Your Daily Values may be higher or lower depending on your calorie needs.

Directions:

1. Preheat oven to 405 F.

2. In a food processor, pulse the chopped cauliflower until a rice-like texture is attained.

3. Microwave the riced cauliflower on high for 5 minutes.

4. Pour out the riced cauliflower on a clean kitchen towel and squeeze out as much water as you can. Repeat the process two more times, allowing the cauliflower to rest between cycles

5. In a large bowl, add the cauliflower paste, egg, coconut flour, and avocado oil. Season with a pinch of salt.

6. Shape the dough into a pizza crust on top of a baking tray lined with parchment paper. Do not spread the crust thinner than 1/4 inch.

7.   Bake the crust for 25 to 30 minutes until it is has developed a golden brown color with light brown edges.

8.   Take out the crust and allow to cool for 10 minutes.

9.   Spread out the tomato puree on top of the crust as evenly as possible.

10.   Top the pizza with shredded mozzarella.

11.   Return the pizza to the oven and bake for another 5 minutes.

Did you know?

Take out the pizza and slice into 4 parts. Serve while hot. Tomatoes are the fruit of the tomato plant. They originated in the South American Andes around the area of modern day Peru and was first used as a food by the Aztec's in Southern Mexico.

Keto Pasta with Blue

Cheese Sauce

INGREDIENTS	Fats	Proteins	Carbs
1 egg	9.64 g	8.97 g	1.02 g
1/8 cup cream cheese	9.93 g	1.72 g	1.18 g
1 tbsp. coconut flour	5.53 g	0.42 g	1.72 g
3 tbsp. cream cheese	12.87 g	3.2 g	1.58 g
1/4 cup blue cheese	9.71 g	7.23 g	0.79 g

Ingredient	Amount		
1 1/2 tbsp. butter	17.28 g	0.18 g	0.01 g
1 tsp. pine nuts	1.91 g	0.38 g	0.37 g
2 tbsp. parmesan, grated	2.78 g	2.84 g	1.39 g

Nutrition Facts

Amount per 220 g
1 serving (7.8 oz)

Calories 749
From fat 614

	Amount	% Daily Value*		Amount	% Daily Value*
Total Fat	69.7g	107%	Total Carbohydrates	8g	3%
Saturated	40.1g	201%	Dietary Fiber	0g	0%
Trans Fat	0.8g		Sugars	3g	
Cholesterol	771mg	257%	Protein	25g	50%
Sodium	977mg	41%			
Calcium 38% • Iron 22%			Vitamin A 44% • Vitamin C		0%

* Percent Daily Values are based on 2000 calorie diet. Your Daily Values may be higher or lower depending on your calorie needs

Directions:

1.	Preheat oven to 300 F.

2.	Whisk together the eggs, cream cheese, and coconut flour. Season with salt. Let the batter rest for 2 minutes.

3.	Line a baking tray with parchment paper. Spread the batter on the parchment paper. Place another piece of parchment paper on top of the batter and flatten using a rolling pin. Continue rolling until the batter is about 1 to 2 mm inches in thickness.

4.   Place the baking tray in the oven (still covered with the parchment paper). Bake for 10 to 12 minutes.

5.   Remove the tray from the oven and let cool. Remove the parchment paper cover.

6.   Using a small knife, cut the pasta into thin strips.

7.   Prepare the sauce. In a small saucepan, melt the butter over low heat.

8.   Add in the cream cheese and blue cheese. Stir until smooth. Cook only until all the cheese has been melted.

9.   Mix the sauce with the pasta. Top with pine nuts and grated parmesan. Serve immediately.

Did you know?

The coconut comes from the coconut palm tree which grows throughout the tropics and subtropics.

DAY 10

Meal	Recipe	Calories
Breakfast	Chai Yogurt Smoothie	518
Lunch	Cheesy Cauliflower Bake	771
Dinner	Keto Salad Nicoise	544

Chai Yogurt Smoothie

INGREDIENTS	Fats	Proteins	Carbs
1/2 tsp. vanilla extract	0 g	0 g	0.27 g
1 cup coconut milk	48.21 g	4.57 g	6.35 g
1 cup brewed chai tea	0 g	0 g	0.71 g
2 tbsp. plain yogurt	0.99 g	1.06 g	1.43 g
1 tbsp. protein powder	1.89 g	5.03 g	2.04 g

Nutrition Facts

Amount per 507 g
1 serving (17.9 oz)

Calories 518
From fat 429

Amount	% Daily Value*	Amount	% Daily Value*
Total Fat 51.1g	79%	Total Carbohydrates 11g	4%
Saturated 43.6g	218%	Dietary Fiber 1g	3%
Trans Fat 0g		Sugars 2g	
Cholesterol 6mg	2%	Protein 11g	21%
Sodium 87mg	4%		
Calcium 13% • Iron 47%		Vitamin A 6% • Vitamin C 10%	

* Percent Daily Values are based on 2000 calorie diet. Your Daily Values may be higher or lower depending on your calorie needs.

Directions:

1.   Add all ingredients in a blender, along with 4 ice cubes.

2.   Blend until smooth.

3.   You may also serve with a pinch of cinnamon or nutmeg, if desired.

Did you know?

The flower that produces the vanilla bean lasts only one day. The beans are hand-picked and then cured, wrapped, and dried in a process that takes 4 to 6 months

Cheesy baked

Cauliflower

Nutrition Facts	Amount	% Daily Value*	Amount	% Daily Value*
	Total Fat 76.5g	118%	Total Carbohydrates 9g	3%
	Saturated 46.1g	230%	Dietary Fiber 2g	7%
Amount per 266 g	Trans Fat 1.3g		Sugars 5g	
1 serving (9.4 oz)	Cholesterol 241mg	80%	Protein 14g	29%
Calories 765	Sodium 655mg	27%		
From fat 675	Calcium 35% • Iron 4%		Vitamin A 59% • Vitamin C 67%	

* Percent Daily Values are based on 2000 calorie diet. Your Daily Values may be higher or lower depending on your calorie needs.

INGREDIENTS	Fats	Proteins	Carbs
3/4 cup cauliflower, chopped	0.22 g	1.54 g	3.99 g
2 tbsp. butter	23.04 g	0.24 g	0.02 g
1/2 cup heavy cream	22.2 g	1.23 g	1.67 g
1/4 cup cream cheese	19.86 g	3.44 g	2.36 g
1/4 cup cheddar, diced	11.16 g	7.93 g	0.44 g
1 tbsp. green onions, sliced	0.03 g	0.06 g	0.34 g

Directions:

1.   Preheat oven to 350 F.

2.   Boil a pot of water. Blanch the chopped cauliflower for 2 minutes and drain immediately.

3.   In a separate pot, melt the butter over medium heat.

4.   To the butter, add the heavy cream, cream cheese, and half of the cheddar. Season with salt and pepper. Stir until everything has melted and has been well-combined.

5.   On a baking dish, combine the cauliflower and cheese sauce. Top with green onions and the remaining cheddar.

6.   Bake for about 30 minutes, or until the top has turned golden brown.

7.   Remove from oven and serve immediately.

Did you know?

Slicing onions make us cry and we really hate that. But why do we cry while cutting onions? That's because, when we cut onions, sulfur is released by the veggie. This sulfur reaches our eyes and combines with the moisture to produce sulfuric acid.

Keto Salad Nicoise

INGREDIENTS	Fats	Proteins	Carbs
1 large egg	4.76 g	6.28 g	0.36 g
1/2 cup celery, chopped	0.04 g	0.17 g	0.75 g
1/2 snow peas	0 g	0.05 g	0.13 g
2 tbsp. olive oil	27 g	0 g	0 g

1/4 tbsp. garlic, chopped	0.01 g	0.13 g	0.69 g
1 cup romaine lettuce, shredded	0.14 g	0.58 g	1.55 g
1/2 tbsp green onion, chopped	0.01 g	0.03 g	0.17 g
1/2 tbsp olives, chopped	0.45 g	0.04 g	0.26 g
1 tbsp. balsamic vinegar	0 g	0.08 g	2.72 g
1/2 cup feta cheese, crumbled	15.96 g	10.66 g	3.07 g

Nutrition Facts

Amount per 251 g
1 serving (8.9 oz)

Calories 544
From fat 427

Amount	% Daily Value*	Amount	% Daily Value*
Total Fat 48.4g	74%	Total Carbohydrates 10g	3%
Saturated 16.6g	83%	Dietary Fiber 2g	7%
Trans Fat 0g		Sugars 7g	
Cholesterol 253mg	84%	Protein 18g	36%
Sodium 819mg	34%		
Calcium 44% • Iron 13%		Vitamin A 99% • Vitamin C 8%	

* Percent Daily Values are based on 2000 calorie diet. Your Daily Values may be higher or lower depending on your calorie needs.

Directions:

1.   In a small pot, boil the egg until hard. Allow to cool, peel, and cut into wedges.

2.   In a small frying pan, sauté the snow peas, olives, and garlic in 1 tbsp. of olive oil. Cook until the snow peas change color to a bright green.

3.   In a large bowl, combine the romaine lettuce, cooked vegetables, green onion, and celery.

4.   Prepare the dressing. Whisk together the olive oil and balsamic vinegar. Season with salt and pepper, if desired.

5.   Add the dressing to the salad. Add the feta cheese.

6.   Toss until the dressing has been fully incorporated. Serve.

Did you know?

Celery is low-energy vegetable. Due to low level of calories, celery is suitable for diets. Celery contains certain amounts of vitamins C, K, B2 and dietary fibers

DAY 11

Meal	Recipe	Calories
Breakfast	Thai-Style Egg Drop Soup	532
Lunch	Spicy Tofu Tacos	614
Dinner	Greek Salad	594

Thai-Style Egg Drop Soup

INGREDIENTS	Fats	Proteins	Carbs
1 1/2 cup vegetable broth	0 g	0 g	4.51 g
1 tbsp. sesame oil	13.6 g	0 g	0 g
1/2 tbsp. fish sauce	0 g	0.46 g	0.33 g
1 tsp. lemon rind	0.01 g	0.03 g	0.32 g
1/2 tbsp. ginger, grated	0.02 g	0.05 g	0.53 g
1/2 tbsp. green onion	0.01 g	0.03 g	0.17 g

1 egg	4.18 g	5.53 g	0.32 g
1/2 cup coconut milk	24.1 g	2.28 g	3.18 g
1 tbsp. butter	11.52 g	0.12 g	0.01 g

Nutrition Facts

Amount per 553 g
1 serving (19.5 oz)

Calories 532
From fat 461

Amount	% Daily Value*	Amount	% Daily Value*
Total Fat 53.4g	82%	Total Carbohydrates 9g	3%
Saturated 32g	160%	Dietary Fiber 0g	1%
Trans Fat 0.5g		Sugars 4g	
Cholesterol 194mg	65%	Protein 8g	17%
Sodium 2196mg	92%		
Calcium 6% • Iron 26%		Vitamin A 28% • Vitamin C	7%

* Percent Daily Values are based on 2000 calorie diet. Your Daily Values may be higher or lower depending on your calorie needs.

Directions:

1.   In a medium-sized pot, heat the vegetable broth with the lemon rind and ginger

2.   Bring the water to a simmer for 15 minutes. Strain the broth to remove the ginger and lemon rind.

3.   Return the broth to the pot. Stir in the coconut milk, sesame oil, and fish sauce. Bring the broth to a simmer.

4.   In a small bowl, whisk together the butter and the eggs.

5.   While stirring the broth, gradually pour in the whisked egg.

6.   Serve while hot. Garnish with green onions.

Did you know?

Consuming ginger roots is the vital boost to the immunity, Aside from treating nausea and throaty coughs, ginger boosts the immune system to protect against viruses like the flu or the common cold.

Spicy Tofu Tacos

INGREDIENTS	Fats	Proteins	Carbs
1 egg	4.18 g	5.53 g	0.32 g
1/2 cup coconut flour	4.9 g	0.38 g	1.53 g
1 tbsp. avocado oil	14 g	0 g	0 g
1 cup romaine lettuce, shredded	0.11 g	0.43 g	1.16 g
1 tbsp. lime juice	0.01 g	0.06 g	1.27 g
1 tbsp. red onion, chopped	0.01 g	0.11 g	0.93 g

1/2 cup firm tofu	5.49 g	9.94 g	2.69 g
1/4tbsp. paprika	0.44 g	0.48 g	0.92 g
2 tbsp. olive oil	27 g	0 g	0 g
1/8 cup avocado, sliced	2.79 g	0.38 g	1.62 g

Nutrition Facts

Amount per 236 g

1 serving (8.3 oz)

Calories 614

From fat 513

	Amount	% Daily Value*	Amount	% Daily Value*
Total Fat 58.7g		90%	Total Carbohydrates 10g	3%
Saturated 12.3g		62%	Dietary Fiber 4g	17%
Trans Fat 0g			Sugars 2g	
Cholesterol 164mg		55%	Protein 17g	34%
Sodium 80mg		3%		
Calcium 48% • Iron 20%			Vitamin A 86% • Vitamin C 15%	

* Percent Daily Values are based on 2000 calorie diet. Your Daily Values may be higher or lower depending on your calorie needs.

Directions:

1.   Preheat the oven to 350 F.

2.   In a small bowl, toss the tofu cubes in olive oil and paprika. Season with salt and pepper, if desired.

3.   Line a baking tray with parchment paper and spread the tofu cubes evenly. Bake in the oven for 25 to 30 minutes, or until the tofu is firm and crispy.

4.   Remove from the oven and set aside.

5.   Prepare the tortillas. Combine the egg, coconut flour, and avocado oil in a small bowl. Mix thoroughly.

6.   Preheat a small frying pan over medium heat. Coat the pan with some avocado oil.

7.   Pour one spoonful of the batter mixture into the pan. Move the pan around to spread the batter mixture to a diameter of 6 to 8 inches.

8.   Once the top of the tortilla has started to firm up, flip the tortilla and cook the other side for a few more seconds.

9.   Repeat until all the tortilla batter has been used up.

10.   In a large bowl, combine the romaine lettuce, avocado slices, and red onion. Add the cooked tofu.

11.   Add the lime juice to the taco filling. Toss to mix.

12.   Assemble the tacos by placing 3 tbsp. of filling to each tortilla. Fold up the tortilla.

13.   Repeat until all the filling or all the tortillas have been used up. Serve and enjoy!

Did you know?

Limes are high in vitamin C, although not as high as lemons, and they have small quantities of many other vitamins and minerals.

Greek Salad

INGREDIENTS	Fats	Proteins	Carbs
1/4 cup tomato, diced	0.09 g	0.4 g	1.75 g

1/4 cup cucumber, sliced	0.05 g	0.18 g	0.64 g
1/4 cup red onion, sliced	0.03 g	0.3 g	2.57 g
1/4 cup bell pepper, sliced	0.02 g	0.23 g	1.07 g
1/2 cup feta cheese, crumbled	15.96 g	10.66 g	3.07 g
1 tbsp. olives, chopped	0.9 g	0.07 g	0.53 g
3 tbsp. olive oil	40.5 g	0 g	0 g
1/2 tbsp. red wine vinegar	0 g	0 g	0.02 g

Nutrition Facts

Amount per 245 g
1 serving (8.6 oz)

Calories 594
From fat 507

Amount	% Daily Value*	Amount	% Daily Value*
Total Fat 57.5g	89%	Total Carbohydrates 10g	3%
Saturated 17g	85%	Dietary Fiber 2g	7%
Trans Fat 0g		Sugars 6g	
Cholesterol 67mg	22%	Protein 12g	24%
Sodium 756mg	32%		
Calcium 40% • Iron 8%		Vitamin A 18% • Vitamin C 61%	

* Percent Daily Values are based on 2000 calorie diet. Your Daily Values may be higher or lower depending on your calorie needs.

Directions:

1.   In a medium-sized bowl, combine the tomato, bell pepper, cucumber, onion, olives, and feta cheese.

2.   Drizzle in the olive oil and vinegar. Season with salt and pepper, if desired.

3.   Toss until thoroughly mixed, making sure that everything is coated with dressing. Serve and enjoy.

Did you know?

The olive is a fruit, not a vegetable. Can be green, purple, dark brown, black, and even pink color.

DAY 12

Meal	Recipe	Calories
Breakfast	No-Grain Granola	746
Lunch	Bell Pepper Nachos	571
Dinner	Tofu and Broccoli Stir Fry	549

No-Grain Granola

INGREDIENTS	Fats	Proteins	Carbs
1/4 cup desiccated coconut	12.43 g	0.95 g	3.87 g
1 tbsp. sunflower seeds	4.53 g	1.83 g	1.76 g
1 tbsp. pumpkin seeds	3.63 g	2.21 g	1.09 g
1/2 tbsp. flaxseed, ground	4.63 g	1.88 g	0.75 g
1 tbsp. walnuts, chopped	0.01 g	0.03 g	0.56 g
1/4 cup coconut oil	54.5 g	0 g	0 g

1/4 tsp cinnamon powder	0.76 g	0.33 g	0.52 g

Nutrition Facts

Amount per 99 g

1 serving (3.5 oz)

Calories 746
From fat 687

	Amount	% Daily Value*	Amount	% Daily Value*
Total Fat 80.5g		124%	Total Carbohydrates 9g	3%
Saturated 59.5g		298%	Dietary Fiber 3g	10%
Trans Fat 0.1g			Sugars 0g	
Cholesterol 0mg		0%	Protein 7g	14%
Sodium 27mg		1%		
Calcium 3% • Iron 12%			Vitamin A 0% • Vitamin C 1%	

* Percent Daily Values are based on 2000 calorie diet. Your Daily Values may be higher or lower depending on your calorie needs.

Directions:

1.   Preheat the oven to 350 F.

2.   In a large baking tray, mix together the desiccated coconut, sunflower seeds, pumpkin seeds, flaxseed, and walnuts.

3.   In a small pan over low heat, melt the coconut oil and mix in the cinnamon powder.

4.   Pour the coconut oil over the granola mix and mix thoroughly. Make sure all the components of the granola mix are coated with the coconut oil

5.   Bake for 20 minutes.

6.   To avoid burning the granola, the mixture needs to be stirred or turned every 3 minutes.

7.   Allow the granola mix to cool to room temperature before serving.

Did you know?

Cinnamon is high in fiber and calcium which helps improve colon health.

Bell Pepper Nachos

INGREDIENTS	Fats	Proteins	Carbs
1 cup bell pepper, sliced	0.16 g	0.79 g	4.27 g
2 tbsp. olive oil	27 g	0 g	0 g
1/4 tsp cumin	0.11 g	0.09 g	0.22 g
1/4 tsp chili powder	0.1 g	0.09 g	0.35 g
1/4 tbsp. jalapeno, sliced	0.04 g	0.09 g	0.65 g
3 tbsp. sour cream	3.82 g	1.26 g	2.56 g

1/4 cup cheddar, shredded	11.16 g	7.93 g	0.44 g
1 tbsp. cilantro	0.01 g	0.02 g	0.04 g
1 tbsp. avocado oil	14 g	0 g	0 g

Directions:

1.   Preheat oven to 350 F.

2.   Place the sliced bell peppers on a baking tray.

3.   Toss the bell peppers with olive oil, avocado oi, cumin, and chili powder. Season with salt, if desired.

4.   Bake the peppers until tender for about 15 to 20 minutes.

5.   Place the cooked bell peppers in a small bowl. Top with shredded cheddar and sliced jalapeno.

6.   Drizzle sour cream over the top and garnish with cilantro. Serve.

Did you know?
Jalapeño peppers are a good source of vitamin C, folate and vitamin A. They are low fat, saturated fat free, cholesterol free, and sodium free.

Tofu and Broccoli

StirFry

Nutrition Facts	Amount	% Daily Value*	Amount	% Daily Value*
	Total Fat 49.9g	77%	Total Carbohydrates 9g	3%
Amount per 198 g	Saturated 6.8g	34%	Dietary Fiber 5g	20%
1 serving (7 oz)	Trans Fat 0g		Sugars 1g	
	Cholesterol 0mg	0%	Protein 23g	46%
Calories 549	Sodium 283mg	12%		
From fat 433	Calcium 91% • Iron 25%		Vitamin A 23% • Vitamin C 7%	
	* Percent Daily Values are based on 2000 calorie diet. Your Daily Values may be higher or lower depending on your calorie needs.			

INGREDIENTS	Fats	Proteins	Carbs
1/2 cup firm tofu cubes	10.99 g	19.88 g	5.38 g
1/2 cup broccoli, chopped	0.1 g	0.63 g	0.57 g
1/2 tbsp. soy sauce	0.02 g	0.61 g	1.08 g
1 tsp sesame seeds	1.65 g	0.55 g	0.32 g
1 tbsp. sesame oil	13.6 g	0 g	0 g
1 1/2 tbsp. olive oil	20.3 g	0 g	0 g
1/2 tsp chili powder	0.2 g	0.19 g	0.7 g
1 tbsp. almond, slivered	3 g	1.27 g	1.29 g

Directions:

1.   Preheat oven to 425 F.

2.   Toss the tofu with 1/2 tbsp. olive oil, salt, and pepper and place on a small baking tray. Make sure the cubes do not touch each other.

3.   Bake the tofu in the oven for 25 to 30 minutes, or until the outsides are firm and crunchy.

4.   Combine the remaining olive oil and sesame oil in a large frying pan and place over high heat.

5.   Add the slivered almonds to the pan and cook for 1 to 2 minutes, or until fragrant.

6.   Add the cooked tofu and stir.

7.   Add the broccoli. Stir while cooking for 4 to 5 minutes, or just until the broccoli has developed a bright green color.

8.   Add in the soy sauce and chili powder. Cook for an additional 1 minutes. .

9.   Transfer to a bowl and garnish with sesame seeds. Serve and enjoy.

Did you know?
Almonds help to slow absorption of sugar and carbs

DAY 13

Meal	Recipe	Calories
Breakfast	Cauliflower Toast	524
Lunch	Spicy Tofu and Eggplant	622
Dinner	Sweet and Sour Mushroom Stir Fry	551

Cauliflower Toast

INGREDIENTS	Fats	Proteins	Carbs
1 egg	4.18 g	5.53 g	0.32 g
1/2 cup cauliflower, chopped	0.15 g	1.03 g	2.66 g
1/2 cup cheddar, shredded	22.32 g	15.87 g	0.88 g
1 tsp garlic powder	0.02 g	0.61 g	2.25 g
4 tbsp. guacamole	4.58 g	0.63 g	2.71 g
1 tbsp. olive oil	13.5 g	0 g	0 g

Directions:

1.   Cook the chopped cauliflower in a steamer for 10 minutes, or until tender.

2.   Place the cooked cauliflower in food processor and pulse until a very fine texture is achieved.

3.   Wrap the ground cauliflower with a clean kitchen towel and squeeze toe remove excess moisture. Let the ground cauliflower rest for around 10 minutes and squeeze out the excess moisture again. Repeat this process one more time.

4.   In a medium-sized bowl, combine the ground cauliflower, egg, cheddar, and garlic powder. Season with salt and pepper.

5.   In a small frying pan, preheat the olive oil over medium heat.

6.   Place the cauliflower batter into the frying pan and form into the shape of a toast. You may divide the batter into two if there is too much.

7.   Cook on one side until firm and golden brown. Flip and resume cooking on the other side.

8.   Transfer the cooked toast on a plate and top with guacamole. Serve.

Did you know?

Cheese is kept for a period of time before it's ready to eat. Some varieties of cheese, blue cheese, Gorgonzola, and brie are exposed to mold, which helps them age properly.

Spicy Tofu and Eggplant

INGREDIENTS	Fats	Proteins	Carbs
1/2 cup firm tofu cubes	10.99 g	19.88 g	5.38 g
1/4 cup eggplant, diced	0.04 g	0.2 g	1.21 g
1 tbsp. green snap beans	0.04 g	0.11 g	0.41 g
1/2 tbsp. soy sauce	0.05 g	0.63 g	0.71 g
1/2 tsp garlic, chopped	0.01 g	0.09 g	0.46 g
2 tbsp. olive oil	27 g	0 g	0 g
1 1/2 tbsp. sesame oil	20.4 g	0 g	0 g
1 tbsp. red chili, chopped	0.04 g	0.15 g	0.7 g
1/4 tbsp. cider vinegar	0 g	0 g	0.03 g

	Nutrition Facts	Amount	% Daily Value*	Amount	% Daily Value*
		Total Fat 58.6g	90%	Total Carbohydrates 9g	3%
		Saturated 8.2g	41%	Dietary Fiber 4g	16%
Amount per 226 g		Trans Fat 0g		Sugars 1g	
1 serving (8 oz)		Cholesterol 0mg	0%	Protein 21g	42%
Calories 620		Sodium 634mg	26%		
From fat 512		Calcium 87% • Iron 21%		Vitamin A 6% • Vitamin C 22%	

* Percent Daily Values are based on 2000 calorie diet. Your Daily Values may be higher or lower depending on your calorie needs.

Directions:

1.   Preheat oven to 425 F.

2.   Toss the tofu with 1/2 tbsp. olive oil, salt, and pepper and place on a small baking tray. Make sure the cubes do not touch each other.

3.   Bake the tofu in the oven for 25 to 30 minutes, or until the outsides are firm and crunchy.

4.   In a large frying pan, preheat the remaining olive oil and sesame oil over high heat.

5.   To the frying pan, add the eggplant and garlic. Cook for 5 to 6 minutes, until soft but not mushy.

6.   Add the cooked tofu and stir.

7.   Add the snap beans to the pan and stir.

8.   Add the soy sauce, cider vinegar, and red chili. Cook for another 2 to 3 minutes.

9.   Transfer to a bowl and serve.

Did you know?
Soy sauce is generally made from soybeans, wheat, salt and water, although tamari, a traditional Japanese soy sauce, usually does not include wheat, which makes it suitable for a gluten free diet.

Sweet and Sour

Mushroom Stir Fry

INGREDIENTS	Fats	Proteins	Carbs
1/2 tbsp. tomato paste	0.04 g	0.35 g	1.51 g
1/2 cup vegetable broth	0 g	0 g	1.5 g
1/4 tbsp. Apple cider vinegar	0 g	0 g	0.03 g
1/4 tbsp. lime juice	0 g	0.02 g	0.32 g
1/2 tbsp. Stevia	0 g	0 g	2 g
1/4 tbsp. fish sauce	0 g	0.23 g	0.16 g
1/4 tbsp. ginger, sliced	0.01 g	0.03 g	0.27 g
1 cup oyster mushrooms, sliced	0.35 g	2.85 g	5.24 g
2 tbsp. olive oil	27 g	0 g	0 g
1 cup broccoli, sliced	0.2 g	1.27 g	1.14 g
2 tbsp. sesame oil	27.2 g	0 g	0 g
1 tsp sesame seeds	1.65 g	0.55 g	0.32 g
1/2 tbsp. green onion, chopped	0.01 g	0.03 g	0.17 g

Nutrition Facts

Amount per 327 g
1 serving (11.5 oz)

Calories 551
From fat 498

	Amount	% Daily Value*	Amount	% Daily Value*
Total Fat	56.5g	87%	Total Carbohydrates 13g	4%
Saturated	7.9g	40%	Dietary Fiber 4g	15%
Trans Fat	0g		Sugars 3g	
Cholesterol	0mg	0%	Protein 5g	11%
Sodium	859mg	36%		
Calcium	6%	• Iron 15%	Vitamin A 32% • Vitamin C	19%

* Percent Daily Values are based on 2000 calorie diet. Your Daily Values may be higher or lower depending on your calorie needs.

Directions:

1. In a medium-sized saucepan, combine the vegetable broth, tomato paste, vinegar, lime juice, fish sauce, Stevia, and ginger. Stir well while heating the mixture to a boil. Boil for 3 minutes, or until thick enough for your liking. Remove from the heat and let cool. Set aside.

2. In a large frying pan, preheat the sesame oil and olive oil.

3. Add the oyster mushrooms to the frying pan and cook for 9 to 10 minutes, or until tender.

4. Add the broccoli and cook for another 4 to 5 minutes, or until the broccoli has turned bright green.

5. Add the sweet and sour sauce and stir thoroughly. Make sure all the pieces of mushroom and broccoli are coated with the sauce.

6. Add in the sesame seeds and green onion. Season with salt and pepper.

7. Turn off the heat and stir thoroughly.

8. Transfer to a bowl and serve.

Did you know?

Stevia leaves contain potassium, zinc, magnesium and vitamin B3. The Mayo Clinic says stevia and other artificial sweeteners may be attractive to people with diabetes because they make food taste sweet without increasing blood sugar level

DAY 14

Meal	Recipe	Calories
Breakfast	Cauliflower Flatbread with Cheese	592
Lunch	Broccoli and Spinach Curry	603
Dinner	Cauliflower Parmesan Soup	575

Cauliflower Flatbread with Cheese

INGREDIENTS	Fats	Proteins	Carbs
1/2 cup cauliflower, chopped	0.15 g	1.03 g	2.66 g
1 egg	4.18 g	5.53 g	0.32 g
1/4 tbsp. garlic, chopped	0.01 g	0.13 g	0.69 g
1/2 tsp dried oregano	0.04 g	0.08 g	0.62 g
3/4 cup mozzarella, shredded	18.77 g	18.62 g	1.84 g
1/4 cup parmesan, grated	6.96 g	7.11 g	3.48 g
1/2 tbsp. parsley	0.02 g	0.06 g	0.12 g

1 1/2 tbsp. butter	17.28 g	0.18 g	0.01 g

Nutrition Facts

Amount per 233 g
1 serving (8.2 oz)

Calories 592
From fat 418

Amount	% Daily Value*	Amount	% Daily Value*
Total Fat 47.4g	73%	**Total Carbohydrates** 10g	3%
Saturated 27.3g	136%	Dietary Fiber 2g	6%
Trans Fat 0.9g		Sugars 2g	
Cholesterol 297mg	99%	**Protein** 33g	65%
Sodium 1060mg	44%		
Calcium 70% • **Iron** 11%		**Vitamin A** 35% • **Vitamin C** 48%	

* Percent Daily Values are based on 2000 calorie diet. Your Daily Values may be higher or lower depending on your calorie needs.

Directions:

1.   Preheat the oven to 425 C.

2.   Cook the chopped cauliflower in a steamer for 10 minutes, or until tender.

3.   Place the cooked cauliflower in food processor and pulse until a very fine texture is achieved.

4.   Wrap the ground cauliflower with a clean kitchen towel and squeeze toe remove excess moisture. Let the ground cauliflower rest for around 10 minutes and squeeze out the excess moisture again. Repeat this process one more time.

5.   In a large bowl, combine the ground cauliflower, butter, egg, dried oregano, garlic, mozzarella, and parmesan. Season with salt and pepper, if desired. Stir all ingredients until thoroughly combined.

6.   Line a large baking tray with parchment paper and transfer the dough mixture. Pat the dough until it's flat, with a thickness of about quarter of an inch.

7.   Bake in the oven for about 25 minutes or until the top is golden brown.

8.   Remove from the oven and allow to cool before serving.

Did you know?
Oregano is high in antioxidant activity, due to a high content of phenolic acids and flavonoids.

Broccoli and Spinach Curry

INGREDIENTS	Fats	Proteins	Carbs
1/2 cup broccoli, chopped	0.1 g	0.63 g	0.57 g
1 cup spinach	0.12 g	0.86 g	1.09 g
2 tbsp. coconut oil	27.2 g	0 g	0 g
1 tbsp. red onion, chopped	0.01 g	0.11 g	0.93 g
1/4 tbsp. garlic, chopped	0.01 g	0.13 g	0.69 g
1/4 tbsp. ginger, grated	0.01 g	0.03 g	0.27 g
1/4 tbsp. fish sauce	0 g	0.23 g	0.16 g
1/4 tbsp. soy sauce	0.01 g	0.31 g	0.55 g

1/4 tbsp. curry powder	0.88 g	0.9 g	3.52 g
3/4 cup coconut milk	36.15 g	3.42 g	4.76 g

Nutrition Facts

Amount per 275 g
1 serving (9.7 oz)

Calories 613
From fat 547

Amount	% Daily Value*	Amount	% Daily Value*
Total Fat 64.5g	99%	Total Carbohydrates 13g	4%
Saturated 55.7g	279%	Dietary Fiber 5g	19%
Trans Fat 0g		Sugars 1g	
Cholesterol 0mg	0%	Protein 7g	13%
Sodium 520mg	22%		
Calcium 12% • Iron 45%		Vitamin A 67% • Vitamin C 26%	

* Percent Daily Values are based on 2000 calorie diet. Your Daily Values may be higher or lower depending on your calorie needs.

Directions:

1.	In a large frying pan, heat up 1 tbsp. of coconut oil over high heat.

2.	Add the broccoli and stir fry just until the broccoli has turned bright green in color, about 3 to 4 minutes. Set aside.

3.	To the same pan, heat the remaining coconut oil.

4.	Add the red onion, garlic, and ginger. Sauté for 2 to 3 minutes or until fragrant.

5.	Add the coconut milk, soy sauce, fish sauce, and curry powder. Stir while the curry mixture heats up.

6.	Allow the curry mixture to boil and lower the heat to a simmer. Simmer for 10 minutes to allow the flavors to develop,

7.   Add the cooked broccoli and stir. Cook for another minute.

8.   Add the spinach leaves. Season with salt and pepper. Stir and allow to cook for another minute.

9.   Turn off the heat and transfer the curry to a bowl. Serve immediately

Did you know?

Curry powder is made primarily of spices, most often turmeric, cumin and coriander, but the mixture also often contains chilli and fenugreek, and sometimes garlic and ginger.

Cauliflower Parmesan Soup

INGREDIENTS	Fats	Proteins	Carbs
2 tbsp. butter	23.04 g	0. 24 g	0.02 g
1/2 tbsp. white onion, chopped	0.01 g	0.06 g	0.47 g
1/2 tbsp. onion leek, chopped	0.01 g	0.04 g	0.4 g
1/2 cup cauliflower, chopped	0.15 g	1.03 g	2.66 g
1/2 cup vegetable broth	0 g	0 g	1.5 g
1/2 cup heavy cream	22.2 g	1.23 g	1.67 g
2tbsp. parmesan, grated	2.78 g	2.84 g	1.39 g
1/4 cup feta, crumbled	7.98 g	5.33 g	1.53 g

Nutrition Facts

Nutrition Facts	Amount	% Daily Value*	Amount	% Daily Value*
Amount per 315 g	Total Fat 56.2g	86%	Total Carbohydrates 10g	3%
1 serving (11.1 oz)	Saturated 35.6g	178%	Dietary Fiber 1g	5%
	Trans Fat 1g		Sugars 6g	
Calories 575	Cholesterol 185mg	62%	Protein 11g	22%
From fat 494	Sodium 1216mg	51%		
	Calcium 33% • Iron 3%		Vitamin A 43% • Vitamin C 45%	

* Percent Daily Values are based on 2000 calorie diet. Your Daily Values may be higher or lower depending on your calorie needs.

Directions:

1.   In a large pot, melt the butter over medium heat.

2.   Add the white onion and onion leek. Stir while cooking until onions are soft.

3.   Add the chopped cauliflower and vegetable broth. Allow to simmer for about 15 minutes, or until the cauliflower becomes very tender.

4.   Transfer the contents of the pot into a blender. Blend until very smooth.

5.   Return the cauliflower soup into the pot.

6.   Add heavy cream and grated parmesan. Simmer for another 10 minutes.

7.   Ladle the soup into a bowl and top with crumbled feta before serving.

Did you know?

Imported feta cheese is usually made with goat's or sheep's milk, as is the original Greek feta cheese.

DAY 15

Meal	Recipe	Calories
Breakfast	High-Protein Yogurt Bowl	376
Lunch	Keto Stuffed Mushrooms	733
Dinner	Asian Zucchini Salad	846

High-Protein Yogurt Bowl

INGREDIENTS	Fats	Proteins	Carbs
1/2 cup plain yogurt	1.99 g	2.13 g	2.86 g
1/2 tbsp. sunflower seeds	2.26 g	0.91 g	0.88 g
1 tbsp. walnuts	5.22 g	1.22 g	1.1 g
1/2 tbsp. chia seeds	1.23 g	0.66 g	1.68 g
1 tbsp. almond butter	8.88 g	3.35 g	3.01 g
1 tbsp. protein powder	0.96 g	4 g	1.76 g
1/4 cup coconut milk	12.05 g	1.14 g	1.59 g

Directions:

1.   In a blender, combine the coconut milk, yogurt, and protein powder. Blend until completely combined.

2.   Transfer the contents of the blender into a bowl. Add the sunflower seeds, walnuts, and chia seeds. Mix thoroughly.

3.   Drizzle with almond oil. Serve and enjoy!

Did you know?

Not only is yogurt a delicious and healthy snack option, it contains high levels of lactic acid that promote healthy skin.

Keto Stuffed Mushrooms

INGREDIENTS	Fats	Proteins	Carbs
3 whole white mushrooms	0.18 g	1.67 g	1.76 g
1/2 cup cream cheese	34.32 g	8.52 g	4.2 g
1/4 cup heavy cream	22.02 g	1.22 g	1.66 g
1 1/2 tbsp. butter	17.28 g	0.18 g	0.01 g
1/4 tbsp. garlic, chopped	0.01 g	0.13 g	0.69 g
1/4 tsp cayenne pepper	0.09 g	0.06 g	0.28 g
1/2 tsp onion powder	0.01 g	0.12 g	0.95 g

Nutrition Facts

Amount per 259 g
1 serving (9.1 oz)

Calories 733
From fat 657

	Amount	% Daily Value*	Amount	% Daily Value*
	Total Fat 73.9g	114%	Total Carbohydrates 10g	3%
	Saturated 46.3g	232%	Dietary Fiber 1g	4%
	Trans Fat 0.7g		Sugars 7g	
	Cholesterol 235mg	78%	Protein 12g	24%
	Sodium 687mg	29%		
	Calcium 14% • Iron 10%		Vitamin A 57% • Vitamin C 5%	

* Percent Daily Values are based on 2000 calorie diet. Your Daily Values may be higher or lower depending on your calorie needs.

Directions:

1.   Slice off the stems of the mushrooms and carve out the insides from the bottom using a paring knife.

2.   In a medium-sized frying pan, melt the butter over medium heat.

3.   Add the mushroom stems, garlic, cayenne pepper, and onion powder. Cook while stirring for 8 to 9 minutes, or until the mushroom stems are tender.

4.   Add the heavy cream and cream cheese to the pan. Allow the mixture to simmer and thicken to your liking.

5.   Remove the pan from the heat and allow to cool. The filling mixture should thicken even more.

6.   Preheat the oven to 375 F.

7.   Carefully spoon the filling into the cavity of each mushroom.

8.   In a small baking tray, arrange the mushrooms side by side. Bake for 25 to 30 minutes.

9.   Allow to cool before serving.

Did you know?

Cayenne peppers are actually hotter when they are more mature, in their red form.

Asian Zucchini Salad

INGREDIENTS	Fats	Proteins	Carbs
1 medium zucchini	0.04 g	0.3 g	0.34 g
1/2 cup cabbage, shredded	0.04 g	0.57 g	2.58 g
1 1/2 tbsp. sunflower seeds	6.74 g	2.72 g	2.62 g
1/2 tbsp. almonds	0.3 g	0.13 g	0.13 g
3 tbsp. avocado oil	42 g	0 g	0 g
1 1/2 tbsp. sesame oil	20.4 g	0 g	0 g
1 tbsp. white vinegar	0 g	0 g	0.14 g
1/2 cup feta cheese, crumbled	15.96 g	10.66 g	3.07 g

Nutrition Facts	Amount	% Daily Value*	Amount	% Daily Value*
Amount per 222 g 1 serving (7.8 oz)	Total Fat 85.5g	132%	Total Carbohydrates 9g	3%
	Saturated 19.6g	98%	Dietary Fiber 2g	10%
	Trans Fat 0g		Sugars 5g	
Calories 846	Cholesterol 67mg	22%	Protein 14g	29%
From fat 752	Sodium 698mg	29%		
	Calcium 40% • Iron 8%		Vitamin A 8% • Vitamin C 34%	

* Percent Daily Values are based on 2000 calorie diet. Your Daily Values may be higher or lower depending on your calorie needs.

Directions:

1.	In a dry frying pan, toast the almonds until fragrant over low heat.

2.	Slice the zucchini into strands using a spiralizer.

3.   In a large bowl, combine the zucchini, cabbage, sunflower seeds, and almonds.

4.   Whisk together the sesame oil, avocado oil, and white vinegar. Pour the dressing on the salad.

5.   Sprinkle crumbled feta cheese on top of the salad.

6.   Toss the salad together until the dressing has been distributed throughout. Serve.

Did you know?
The term "vinegar" comes from the French word "vin aigre," meaning sour wine.

DAY 16

Meal	Recipe	Calories
Breakfast	Coconut and Walnut Porridge	626
Lunch	Keto Cream of Mushroom Soup	666
Dinner	Pecan Salad with Tahini and Lemon Dressing	555

Coconut and Walnut Porridge

INGREDIENTS	Fats	Proteins	Carbs
1/2 cup coconut milk	24.1 g	2.28 g	3.18 g
1 tbsp. almond butter	8.88 g	3.35 g	3.01 g
3 tbsp. walnuts, crushed	13.88 g	5.63 g	2.24 g
1 1/2 tbsp. desiccated coconut	4.14 g	0.32 g	1.29 g
1/4 tsp cinnamon	0.01 g	0.03 g	0.56 g
1 tbsp. coconut oil	13.6 g	0 g	0 g

Nutrition Facts

Amount per 173 g
1 serving (6.1 oz)

Calories 626
From fat 544

Amount	% Daily Value*	Amount	% Daily Value*
Total Fat 64.6g	99%	Total Carbohydrates 10g	3%
Saturated 38.3g	191%	Dietary Fiber 4g	14%
Trans Fat 0g		Sugars 1g	
Cholesterol 0mg	0%	Protein 12g	23%
Sodium 19mg	1%		
Calcium 10% • Iron 29%		Vitamin A 0% • Vitamin C	3%

* Percent Daily Values are based on 2000 calorie diet. Your Daily Values may be higher or lower depending on your calorie needs.

Directions:

1.   In a saucepan, combine the coconut milk, almond butter, and coconut oil.

2.   Heat the mixture over a stove until boiling.

3.   Add chopped walnuts and desiccated coconut to the saucepan.

4.   Mix thoroughly and remove from heat.

5.   Let the mixture cool down for 5 minutes before transferring to a bowl. Serve.

Did you know?

Coconut os contain median chain triglycerides which are easy to digest. The oil is source of energy and has an accelerating effect on the metabolism.

Keto Cream of Mushroom

Soup

INGREDIENTS	Fats	Proteins	Carbs
1/2 cup cauliflower	0.15 g	1.03 g	2.66 g
1 tbsp. olive oil	13.5 g	0 g	0 g
1 cup white mushroom, sliced	0.24 g	2.16 g	2.28 g
2 tbsp. butter	23.04 g	0.24 g	0.02 g
1/4 tbsp. white onion, chopped	0 g	0.03 g	0.23 g
3/4 cup heavy cream	33.3 g	1.85 g	2.51 g
1/4 cup vegetable broth	0 g	0 g	0.75 g

Nutrition Facts

Amount per 317 g
1 serving (11.2 oz)

Calories 666
From fat 618

Amount	% Daily Value*	Amount	% Daily Value*
Total Fat 70.2g	108%	Total Carbohydrates 8g	3%
Saturated 37.3g	186%	Dietary Fiber 2g	7%
Trans Fat 0.9g		Sugars 6g	
Cholesterol 184mg	61%	Protein 5g	11%
Sodium 472mg	20%		
Calcium 8% • Iron 4%		Vitamin A 43% • Vitamin C 47%	

* Percent Daily Values are based on 2000 calorie diet. Your Daily Values may be higher or lower depending on your calorie needs.

Directions:

1.   In a large pot, combine the cauliflower, vegetable broth, and heavy cream.

2.   Bring to a boil and lower the heat to a simmer. Allow to cook for 7 to 8 minutes, or until the cauliflower is tender.

3.   Transfer the contents of the pot into a blender. Blend the mixture until smooth.

4.   In a large saucepan, melt the butter over high heat. Add the olive oil.

5.   Add the white onions. Stir while cooking until the onions are translucent.

6.   Add the white mushroom and cook while stirring until the mushrooms have turned a light brown, or about 9 to 10 minutes.

7.   Add the cauliflower puree to the mushrooms. Stir thoroughly.

8.   Allow to cook for an additional 10 minutes.

9.   Ladle the soup into a bowl and serve while hot.

Did you know?

There are more amino acids in mushrooms than in corn, peanuts, or soybeans.

Pecan Salad with Tahini and Lemon Dressing

INGREDIENTS	Fats	Proteins	Carbs
1/4 tbsp. tahini	2.04 g	0.65 g	0.81 g
1/4 tbsp. lemon juice	0.01 g	0.01 g	0.26 g
1/2 tbsp. Dijon mustard	0.26 g	0.29 g	0.45 g
1/4 tbsp. garlic, chopped	0 g	0.04 g	0.23 g
1 1/2 tbsp. olive oil	20.3 g	0 g	0 g
1/4 tbsp. rosemary leaves	0.02 g	0.01 g	0.08 g
1 cup romaine lettuce, shredded	0.14 g	0.58 g	1.55 g
2 tbsp. pecans, crushed	11.52 g	1.47 g	2.22 g
1/4 cup celery, sliced	0.04 g	0.17 g	0.75 g
1 tbsp. olives, sliced	0.9 g	0.07 g	0.53 g
1/4 cup gouda, crumbled	16.46 g	14.96 g	1.33 g

Directions:

1. Prepare the dressing. In a blender, combine the tahini, lemon juice, Dijon mustard, garlic, olive oil, and rosemary leaves

2. Blend until smooth. Set aside.

3. In large bowl, combine the lettuce, celery, pecans, olives, and gouda.

4. Drizzle the salad with the dressing.

5. Toss the salad until the dressing is well-distributed.

6. Serve and enjoy.

Did you know?

It has 20% complete protein, making it a higher protein source than most nuts.

DAY 17

Meal	Recipe	Calories
Breakfast	High Protein Chocolate Smoothie	543
Lunch	Corned Tofu with Cabbage	595
Dinner	Keto Shepherd's Pie	688

High Protein Chocolate Smoothie

INGREDIENTS	Fats	Proteins	Carbs
1/2 cup coconut milk	24.1 g	2.28 g	3.18 g
2 tbsp. avocado, cubed	2.35 g	0.32 g	1.36 g
1/2 tbsp. cacao powder, unsweetened	1.71 g	0.31 g	1.84 g
1/4 tsp cinnamon powder	0.01 g	0.03 g	0.56 g
1/4 tsp vanilla extract	0 g	0 g	0.14 g
1 1/2 tbsp. coconut oil	20.4 g	0 g	0 g
2 tbsp. milk-based protein powder	3.77 g	10.06 g	4.07 g

Directions:

1.   Combine all ingredients in a blender. Add 3 ice cubes.

2.   Blend until smooth.

3.   Serve!

Nutrition Facts

Amount per 177 g
1 serving (6.3 oz)

Calories 543
From fat 447

Amount	% Daily Value*	Amount	% Daily Value*
Total Fat 52.3g	81%	**Total Carbohydrates** 11g	4%
Saturated 40.7g	203%	Dietary Fiber 3g	14%
Trans Fat 0g		Sugars 2g	
Cholesterol 5mg	2%	**Protein** 13g	26%
Sodium 89mg	4%		
Calcium 14% • **Iron** 35%		**Vitamin A** 12% • **Vitamin C** 16%	

* Percent Daily Values are based on 2000 calorie diet. Your Daily Values may be higher or lower depending on your calorie needs.

Did you know?

It takes 5 years for a cocoa tree to produce its first seed pods.

Corned Tofu with Cabbage

INGREDIENTS	Fats	Proteins	Carbs
1/4 cup firm tofu, diced	5.49 g	9.94 g	2.69 g
1/4 cup vegetable broth	0 g	0 g	0.75 g
1/2 tbsp. soy sauce	0.05 g	0.65 g	0.39 g
1/4 tbsp. yellow mustard	0.13 g	0.15 g	0.23 g
1/4 tbsp. coriander	0 g	0 g	0 g
1/4 tbsp. ginger, grated	0 g	0.01 g	0.09 g
2 tbsp. olive oil	27 g	0 g	0 g
1/2 cup cabbage, chopped	0.07 g	0.64 g	3.28 g
1/4 tbsp. green onion, chopped	0.01 g	0.01 g	0.09 g
2 tbsp. sesame oil	27.2 g	0 g	0 g

Nutrition Facts

Nutrition Facts	Amount	% Daily Value*	Amount	% Daily Value*
Amount per 235 g	**Total Fat** 60g	92%	**Total Carbohydrates** 8g	3%
1 serving (8.3 oz)	Saturated 8.4g	42%	Dietary Fiber 3g	10%
	Trans Fat 0g		Sugars 2g	
Calories 595	**Cholesterol** 0mg	0%	**Protein** 11g	23%
From fat 527	**Sodium** 739mg	31%		
	Calcium 46% • **Iron** 13%		**Vitamin A** 16% • **Vitamin C** 43%	

* Percent Daily Values are based on 2000 calorie diet. Your Daily Values may be higher or lower depending on your calorie needs.

Directions:

1.   In a small bowl, mix together the vegetable broth, sesame oil, soy sauce, yellow mustard, coriander, and ginger.

2.   Transfer the contents of the bowl into a resealable plastic bag. Add the tofu cubes into the bag.

3.   Place the bag in the refrigerator and allow to marinate for at least 2 hours.

4.   After marinating, remove the tofu cubes from the marinade. Set aside the marinade solution.

5.   Preheat the oven to 425 F.

6.   Line a baking tray with parchment paper and spread the tofu cubes evenly. Bake in the oven for 25 to 30 minutes, or until the tofu is firm and crispy.

7.   Remove from the oven and set aside.

8.   In a large saucepan, heat the olive oil over high heat.

9.   Add the cabbage to the saucepan. Add 2 tbsp. of the marinade solution to the cabbage. Stir while cooking until the cabbage turn bright green but is still crispy.

10.   Toss in the green onions. Stir and remove from heat.

11.   Serve the tofu with the cabbage on the side.

Did you know?

Mustard is made from the ground seeds of a mustard plant, water, vinegar, and optionally some flavorings and spices.

Keto Shepherd's Pie

INGREDIENTS	Fats	Proteins	Carbs
1/4 cup cauliflower, chopped	0.08 g	0.51 g	1.33 g
2 1/2 tbsp. olive oil	33.8 g	0 g	0 g
1/4 tbsp. green onion, chopped	0.01 g	0.01 g	0.09 g
1/4 tbsp. celery, chopped	0 g	0.01 g	0.06 g
1/4 tbsp. garlic	0.01 g	0.13 g	0.69 g
1/4 cup oyster mushrooms, chopped	0.09 g	0.71 g	1.31 g
1/2 tbsp. tomato paste	0.04 g	0.35 g	1.51 g
1/2 cup vegetable broth	0 g	0 g	1.5 g
1/4 tbsp. mustard	0.13 g	0.15 g	0.23 g
1/2 tsp thyme	0.01 g	0.02 g	0.1 g
1/4 cup white mushrooms, chopped	0.06 g	0.54 g	0.57 g
1 egg	4.18 g	5.53 g	0.32 g
2 tbsp. butter	23.04 g	0.24 g	0.02 g
1/4 tsp nutmeg	0.22 g	0.04 g	0.3 g
1/4 cup parmesan, shredded	5.47 g	7.57 g	0.68 g

Nutrition Facts

Amount per 328 g
1 serving (11.6 oz)

Calories 688
From fat 592

Amount	% Daily Value*	Amount	% Daily Value*
Total Fat 67.1g	103%	Total Carbohydrates 9g	3%
Saturated 24.3g	122%	Dietary Fiber 2g	8%
Trans Fat 1g		Sugars 4g	
Cholesterol 239mg	80%	Protein 16g	32%
Sodium 1118mg	47%		
Calcium 30% • Iron 11%		Vitamin A 32% • Vitamin C 28%	

* Percent Daily Values are based on 2000 calorie diet. Your Daily Values may be higher or lower depending on your calorie needs.

Directions:

1.   Preheat the oven to 400 F.

2.   Cook the chopped cauliflower in a steamer for 10 minutes, or until tender.

3.   Place the cooked cauliflower in food processor and pulse until a very fine texture is achieved.

4.   Wrap the ground cauliflower with a clean kitchen towel and squeeze toe remove excess moisture. Let the ground cauliflower rest for around 10 minutes and squeeze out the excess moisture again. Repeat this process one more time.

5.   In a food processor, combine the ground cauliflower, 2 tbsp. olive oil, mustard, thyme, parmesan, and nutmeg. Season with salt and pepper, if desired. Blend until smooth. Set aside.

6.   In a large saucepan, melt the butter over high heat. Add the remaining olive oil.

7.   Add the oyster mushrooms and the white mushrooms to the saucepan. Cook while stirring for 12 to 13 minutes.

8.   Add the garlic and celery. Cook for an additional 4 to 5 minutes.

9.   Add the vegetable broth and celery. Allow to boil and simmer for 15 minutes, or until the volume of the stock has reduced by half.

10.   Add the green onions and stir. Remove the saucepan from the heat.

11.   Assemble the shepherd's pie. Spoon the mushroom stew into a ramekin and top with the cauliflower mash.

12.   Bake the shepherd's pie in the oven for 20 minutes, or until the top has turned a light brown.

13.   Allow to cool for a few minutes before serving.

Did you know?

Thyme was used for soothing of the wounds and for the prevention of infections in the past. It was also used in a treatment of cough, congestion, stomach pain and gout.

DAY 18

Meal	Recipe	Calories
Breakfast	Cauliflower and Parmesan Hash Browns	573
Lunch	Coconut Curry Soup	556
Dinner	Cauliflower and Green Tea Soup	750

Cauliflower and Parmesan Hash Browns

INGREDIENTS	Fats	Proteins	Carbs
1/2 cup cauliflower, chopped	0.15 g	1.03 g	2.66 g
2 tbsp. coconut oil	27.2 g	0 g	0 g
1/2 tbsp. chickpea flour	0.19 g	0.65 g	1.68 g
1/2 tbsp. cornstarch	0 g	0.01 g	3.65 g
1 egg	4.18 g	5.53 g	0.32 g
1 1/2 tbsp. butter	17.28 g	0.18 g	0.01 g
4 tbsp. parmesan, shredded	5.47 g	7.57 g	0.68 g

Nutrition Facts

Amount per 173 g
1 serving (6.1 oz)

Calories 573
From fat 475

Amount	% Daily Value*	Amount	% Daily Value*
Total Fat 54.5g	84%	Total Carbohydrates 9g	3%
Saturated 39.4g	197%	Dietary Fiber 1g	6%
Trans Fat 0.8g		Sugars 2g	
Cholesterol 224mg	75%	Protein 15g	30%
Sodium 422mg	18%		
Calcium 29% • Iron 7%		Vitamin A 19% • Vitamin C 43%	

* Percent Daily Values are based on 2000 calorie diet. Your Daily Values may be higher or lower depending on your calorie needs.

Directions:

1.   Preheat the oven to 400 F.

2.   Cook the chopped cauliflower in a steamer for 10 minutes, or until tender.

3.   Place the cooked cauliflower in food processor and pulse until a very fine texture is achieved.

4.   Wrap the ground cauliflower with a clean kitchen towel and squeeze toe remove excess moisture. Let the ground cauliflower rest for around 10 minutes and squeeze out the excess moisture again. Repeat this process one more time.

5.   In a large bowl, combine the ground cauliflower, chickpea flour, cornstarch, egg, parmesan, coconut oil. Mix thoroughly until well-combined.

6.   Line a baking tray with parchment paper. Scoop a portion of the cauliflower mash into the baking tray and shape into roughly an oval shape. Repeat this until all the cauliflower mash has been consumed.

7.   Bake the patties for 40 minutes or until golden brown and firm. Flip all the patties and bake for another 4 to 5 minutes on the other side.

8.   Place a pat of butter on top of each patty and return to the oven for another 4 to 5 minutes.

9.   Allow to cool for a few minutes before serving.

Did you know?

Chickpea is rich source of dietary fibers and proteins. It contains vitamins B6 and B9 and minerals such as iron and magnesium.

Coconut Curry Soup

INGREDIENTS	Fats	Proteins	Carbs
2 tbsp. coconut oil	27.2 g	0 g	0 g
1/4 tbsp. red onion, chopped	0 g	0.03 g	0.23 g
1/4 tbsp. garlic, chopped	0.01 g	0.13 g	0.69 g
1/4 tbsp. ginger, sliced	0.01 g	0.03 g	0.27 g
1/2 tbsp. curry powder	0.45 g	0.46 g	1.79 g
1/2 cup vegetable broth	0 g	0 g	1.5 g
1/4 cup coconut milk	12.05 g	1.14 g	1.59 g
1/2 tbsp. bell pepper, sliced	0.01 g	0.08 g	0.38 g
1/4 cup white mushrooms, whole	0.08 g	0.74 g	0.78 g
1/2 tbsp. fish sauce	0 g	0.46 g	0.33 g
1/4 tbsp. cilantro	0 g	0.01 g	0.01 g

1/2 medium-sized zucchini	0.02 g	0.15 g	0.17 g
1/2 soft tofu, cubes	4.58 g	8.12 g	2.23 g
1/ tbsp. butter	11.52 g	0.12 g	0.01 g

Nutrition Facts

Amount per 392 g
1 serving (13.8 oz)

Calories 556
From fat 480

Amount	% Daily Value*	Amount	% Daily Value*
Total Fat 55.9g	86%	Total Carbohydrates 10g	3%
Saturated 42.2g	211%	Dietary Fiber 2g	10%
Trans Fat 0.5g		Sugars 3g	
Cholesterol 31mg	10%	Protein 11g	23%
Sodium 1200mg	50%		
Calcium 18% • Iron 23%		Vitamin A 14% • Vitamin C 23%	

* Percent Daily Values are based on 2000 calorie diet. Your Daily Values may be higher or lower depending on your calorie needs.

Directions:

1.   In a large saucepan, melt the coconut oil over high heat. Add the red onion, ginger, garlic, and curry paste. Cook for 3 to 4 minutes until fragrant.

2.   Add the white mushrooms. Stir while cooking for 9 to 10 minutes, or until the mushrooms have developed a light brown color.

3.   Add the vegetable broth and coconut milk. Allow to boil and simmer for 20 minutes.

4.   Add the bell peppers and tofu. Stir and continue simmering for an additional 5 minutes.

5.   Meanwhile, slice the zucchini into thin strip using a spiralizer. Place the zucchini strips in a medium-sized bowl.

6.   Add butter to the curry and stir in to melt. Cook for an additional 2 to 3 minutes.

7.   Ladle the curry over the zucchini. Garnish with some cilantro. Serve while hot.

Did you know?

Cilantro is rich in several vitamins like A, C and K. Vitamin A is an antioxidant and is important for healthy eyes, teeth and skin as well as cell growth and a strong immune system. Vitamin C, a powerful antioxidant, helps boost your immune system, keeps your skin healthy, and is essential for tissue repair and wound healing. Vitamin K is essential for normal blood clotting and is important for bone health

Cauliflower and Green Tea Soup

INGREDIENTS	Fats	Proteins	Carbs
1/4 cup cauliflower, chopped	0.08 g	0.51 g	1.33 g
1 tbsp. leeks, chopped	0.02 g	0.08 g	0.79 g
1/4 tbsp. garlic, chopped	0.01 g	0.13 g	0.69 g
1 tbsp. celery, chopped	0.01 g	0.05 g	0.22 g
1 cup brewed green tea	0 g	0 g	0.47 g
1/4 cup heavy cream	11.1 g	0.62 g	0.84 g
1/2 tbsp. thyme	0.02 g	0.07 g	0.29 g
1/2 tbsp. lemon juice	0.02 g	0.03 g	0.52 g

2 1/2 tbsp. coconut oil	34 g	0 g	0 g
1 tbsp. butter	23.04 g	0.24 g	0.02 g
2 tbsp. almonds, slivered	7.99 g	3.38 g	3.45 g
1/4 cup soft tofu, cubes	2.29 g	4.06 g	1.12 g

Nutrition Facts

Amount per 458 g
1 serving (16.2 oz)

Calories 750
From fat 680

Amount	% Daily Value*	Amount	% Daily Value*
Total Fat 78.6g	121%	Total Carbohydrates 10g	3%
Saturated 51.9g	260%	Dietary Fiber 3g	12%
Trans Fat 1g		Sugars 3g	
Cholesterol 102mg	34%	Protein 9g	18%
Sodium 38mg	2%		
Calcium 16% • Iron 11%		Vitamin A 27% • Vitamin C 33%	

* Percent Daily Values are based on 2000 calorie diet. Your Daily Values may be higher or lower depending on your calorie needs

Directions:

1.   In a large saucepan, melt the coconut oil and butter over high heat.

2.   Add the leeks and garlic and sauté for 5 minutes.

3.   Add the celery, tofu, cauliflower, and lemon juice. Sauté for another 5 minutes.

4.   Add in the green tea and the cream. Sprinkle with thyme and stir.

5.   Bring to a boil and simmer the soup for 20 minutes.

6.   Transfer the contents of the pot to a blender. Puree until smooth.

7.   Ladle to a bowl and top with slivered almonds. Serve while warm.

Did you know?
Lemons are a hybrid between a sour orange and a citron.

DAY 19

Meal	Recipe	Calories
Breakfast	Baked Eggs in Avocado	572
Lunch	Pesto Roasted Cabbage and Mushrooms	576
Dinner	Broccoli in Creamy Blue Cheese Sauce	642

Baked Eggs in Avocado

INGREDIENTS	Fats	Proteins	Carbs
1/2 avocado	14.73 g	2.01 g	8.57 g
1 egg	4.18 g	5.53 g	0.32 g
1/2 cup cheddar, shredded	19.11 g	13.58 g	0.75 g
1 tbsp. olive oil	13.5 g	0 g	0 g

Nutrition Facts	Amount	% Daily Value*	Amount	% Daily Value*
Amount per 215 g	Total Fat 51.5g	79%	Total Carbohydrates 10g	3%
1 serving (7.6 oz)	Saturated 16.3g	82%	Dietary Fiber 7g	27%
	Trans Fat 0.7g		Sugars 1g	
Calories 572	Cholesterol 221mg	74%	Protein 21g	42%
From fat 452	Sodium 434mg	18%		
	Calcium 42% • Iron 8%		Vitamin A 19% • Vitamin C 17%	

* Percent Daily Values are based on 2000 calorie diet. Your Daily Values may be higher or lower depending on your calorie needs.

Directions:

1.   Preheat the oven to 425 C.

2.   Remove the pit from the half avocado.

3.   Carve out just enough of the insides of the avocado to form a crevice for the egg.

4.   Drizzle the open face of the avocado with olive oil and spread it around as much as possible.

5.   Crack open the egg into the avocado.

6.   Sprinkle shredded cheddar on top.

7.   Bake in the oven for 15 to 16 minutes, depending on your desired consistency of the egg.

8.   Serve immediately.

DID YOU KNOW? Avocado trees do not self-pollinate; they need another avocado tree close by in order to grow

Pesto Roasted Cabbage and Mushrooms

INGREDIENTS	Fats	Proteins	Carbs
3/4 cup cabbage, shredded	0.11 g	0.96 g	4.92 g
2 tbsp. pesto sauce	17.6 g	3.13 g	1.28 g
2 tbsp. parmesan, grated	2.78 g	2.84 g	1.39 g
1/4 cup feta, crumbled	7.98 g	5.33 g	1.53 g
1 tbsp. basil, chopped	0.02 g	0.09 g	0.07 g
2 tbsp. olive oil	27 g	0 g	0 g
1/4 cup white mushrooms, chopped	0.06 g	0.54 g	0.57 g

Nutrition Facts

Amount per 192 g
1 serving (6.8 oz)

Calories 576
From fat 488

	Amount	% Daily Value*	Amount	% Daily Value*
Total Fat	55.6g	85%	Total Carbohydrates 10g	3%
Saturated	13.9g	69%	Dietary Fiber 2g	8%
Trans Fat	0.1g		Sugars 5g	
Cholesterol	47mg	16%	Protein 13g	26%
Sodium	832mg	35%		
Calcium	38% • Iron 10%		Vitamin A 30% • Vitamin C	67%

* Percent Daily Values are based on 2000 calorie diet. Your Daily Values may be higher or lower depending on your calorie needs.

Directions:

1.   Preheat the oven to 375 F.

2.   Place the cabbage and chopped mushrooms on a baking tray. Drizzle with olive oil and toss together, ensuring that every piece is coated with oil.

3.   Slather the top with pesto sauce, distributing the sauce as evenly as possible.

4.   Sprinkle parmesan over the top.

5.   Bake in the oven for 20 minutes.

6.   Remove from the oven and sprinkle feta and basil over the top. Serve hot.

Did you know?
Fresh basil's flavor has a clove accent while dried basil has a curry-like flavor

Broccoli in Creamy Blue Cheese Sauce

INGREDIENTS	Fats	Proteins	Carbs
1/4 cup avocado, diced	5.5 g	0.75 g	3.2 g
1/2 tbsp. avocado oil	7 g	0 g	0 g
1 tsp lemon juice	0.01 g	0.02 g	0.35 g
1/4 tsp garlic powder	0.01 g	0.13 g	0.58 g
1/4 tsp tarragon	0.01 g	0.05 g	0.1 g
1 tbsp. heavy cream	5.55 g	0.31 g	0.42 g

1/2 cup broccoli	0.1 g	0.63 g	0.57 g
1 tbsp. olive oil	13.5 g	0 g	0 g
1 tbsp. butter	11.52 g	0.12 g	0.01 g
1/2 cup blue cheese, crumbled	19.4 g	14.45 g	1.58 g

Nutrition Facts

Amount per 181 g
1 serving (6.4 oz)

Calories 642
From fat 549

Amount	% Daily Value*	Amount	% Daily Value*
Total Fat 62.6g	96%	Total Carbohydrates 7g	2%
Saturated 26.8g	134%	Dietary Fiber 3g	13%
Trans Fat 0.5g		Sugars 1g	
Cholesterol 102mg	34%	Protein 16g	33%
Sodium 791mg	33%		
Calcium 40% • Iron 6%		Vitamin A 33% • Vitamin C 17%	

* Percent Daily Values are based on 2000 calorie diet. Your Daily Values may be higher or lower depending on your calorie needs.

Directions:

1.   Prepare the sauce. In a food processor, combine the avocado, avocado oil, butter, lemon juice, heavy cream, garlic powder, blue cheese, and tarragon. Season with salt and pepper, if desired.

2.   Blend until smooth.

3.   In a small flying pan, preheat the olive oil over medium heat.

4.   Add the broccoli florets and stir while cooking for 6 to 7 minutes, or until the broccoli is tender but not soft.

5.   Remove the broccoli from heat. Combine with the creamy avocado sauce and serve while hot.

Did you know?

Leaves of tarragon have sharp, peppery, anise-like flavor. They are rich source of vitamins A and C and minerals such as iodine, calcium, manganese and iron.

DAY 20

Meal	Recipe	Calories
Breakfast	Mushroom Omelet	599
Lunch	Cauliflower Curry Soup with Tofu	638
Dinner	Keto Pesto Gnocchi	672

Mushroom Omelet

INGREDIENTS	Fats	Proteins	Carbs
1 egg	4.18 g	5.53 g	0.32 g
1 1/2 tbsp. butter	17.28 g	0.18 g	0.01 g
1/2 cup cheddar	22.32 g	15.87 g	0.88 g
1 tbsp. green onion, chopped	0.03 g	0.06 g	0.34 g
1/4 cup white mushroom, chopped	0.16 g	1.48 g	1.56 g
2 tbsp. heavy cream	11.1 g	0.62 g	0.84 g

Nutrition Facts

Amount per 215 g
1 serving (7.6 oz)

Calories 599
From fat 490

Amount	% Daily Value*	Amount	% Daily Value*
Total Fat 55.1g	85%	Total Carbohydrates 4g	1%
Saturated 32g	160%	Dietary Fiber 1g	2%
Trans Fat 1.5g		Sugars 2g	
Cholesterol 318mg	106%	Protein 24g	47%
Sodium 639mg	27%		
Calcium 50% • Iron 6%		Vitamin A 42% • Vitamin C 3%	

* Percent Daily Values are based on 2000 calorie diet. Your Daily Values may be higher or lower depending on your calorie needs.

Directions:

1. In a small bowl, whisk together the egg and heavy cream. Season with salt and pepper, if desired

2. In a small pan, melt the 1/2 tbsp. butter over medium heat.

3. Add the white mushroom to the pan. Cook with continuous stirring until the mushroom has turned light brown, about 7 minutes.

4.	To the same pan, add the whisked egg mixture

5.	Add the shredded cheddar and stir.

6.	To keep the omelet runny, stir the mixture as soon as the bottom starts to get firm. Repeat this step until you achieve your desired consistency.

7.	Garnish with green onions before serving.

Did you know?

Butter has a melting temperature of 98.6°F, exactly the same temperature inside the mouth (at least for 99.7% of us). This is what gives butter its rich, creamy feel in the mouth.

Cauliflower Curry Soup with Tofu

INGREDIENTS	Fats	Proteins	Carbs
1/4 cup cauliflower, chopped	0.08 g	0.51 g	1.33 g
1/2 tsp cumin	0.24 g	0.2 g	0.49 g
1/2 tsp paprika	0.15 g	0.17 g	0.65 g

1/2 tsp curry powder	0.14 g	0.14 g	0.56 g
1/2 tsp garlic powder	0.01 g	0.26 g	1.16 g
1 1/2 tbsp. olive oil	20.3 g	0 g	0 g
1 1/2 tbsp. butter	17.28 g	0.18 g	0.01 g
1/2 cup heavy cream	22.2 g	1.23 g	1.67 g
1/2 cup soft tofu, diced	4.58 g	8.12 g	2.23 g

Nutrition Facts

Amount per 257 g
1 serving (9.1 oz)

Calories 638
From fat 570

Amount	% Daily Value*	Amount	% Daily Value*
Total Fat 65g	100%	Total Carbohydrates 8g	3%
Saturated 28.3g	142%	Dietary Fiber 2g	8%
Trans Fat 0.7g		Sugars 3g	
Cholesterol 128mg	43%	Protein 11g	22%
Sodium 48mg	2%		
Calcium 21% • Iron 16%		Vitamin A 41% • Vitamin C 23%	

* Percent Daily Values are based on 2000 calorie diet. Your Daily Values may be higher or lower depending on your calorie needs.

Directions:

1.   Preheat the oven to 425 F.

2.   In a small bowl, toss together the chopped cauliflower, paprika, cumin, curry powder, garlic powder, and olive oil.

3.   Place the seasoned cauliflower on a large baking tray and bake in the oven for about 20 minutes.

4.   Remove from the oven and allow to cool.

5.   Place the cauliflower inside the food processor and pulse until you get a rice-like texture. Set aside.

6.   In a large saucepan, heat the heavy cream with the butter.

7. Add the riced cauliflower and stir. Allow the mixture to boil and simmer for 5 minutes.

8. Add the tofu and stir. Simmer for an additional 10 minutes.

9. Ladle the soup into a bowl and serve while hot.

Did you know?
Cumin is the second most popular spice in the world (black pepper is number one).

Keto Pesto Gnocchi

INGREDIENTS	Fats	Proteins	Carbs
2 egg yolks	9.02 g	5.39 g	1.22 g
1 cup mozzarella, shredded	0 g	35.82 g	3.96 g
1 tsp garlic powder	0.02 g	0.51 g	2.25 g
1 tbsp. butter	11.52 g	0.12 g	0.01 g
1 tbsp. olive oil	13.5 g	0 g	0 g
2 tbsp. pesto sauce	17.6 g	3.13 g	1.28 g

Nutrition Facts

Amount per 208 g
1 serving (7.3 oz)

Calories 672
From fat 456

Amount	% Daily Value*	Amount	% Daily Value*
Total Fat 51.7g	79%	Total Carbohydrates 9g	3%
Saturated 15.4g	77%	Dietary Fiber 3g	10%
Trans Fat 0.5g		Sugars 2g	
Cholesterol 425mg	142%	Protein 45g	90%
Sodium 1238mg	52%		
Calcium 121% • Iron 12%		Vitamin A 35% • Vitamin C 2%	

* Percent Daily Values are based on 2000 calorie diet. Your Daily Values may be higher or lower depending on your calorie needs.

Directions:

1.   Melt the mozzarella in the microwave.

2.   Combine the egg yolks, melted mozzarella, and garlic powder. Mix until a dough-like consistency is achieved.

3.   Divide the dough into 2 portions.

4.   Chill the dough in the refrigerator for 10 minutes.

5.   Line a baking tray with parchment paper. Lightly grease the surface with some olive oil.

6.   Roll out each dough into 1/2-inch thick logs.

7.   Slice each log into 1-inch pieces.

8.   In a large pot, bring some salted water to a boil. Drop the gnocchi pieces into the boiling water.

9.   You will know that the gnocchi are done cooking when they float, which should take about 2 to 3 minutes. Strain the cooked gnocchi using a colander.

10.   In a large frying pan, melt the butter in the olive oil over medium heat.

11.   Add the gnocchi and sauté for about 2 to 3 minutes, or until they turn golden brown.

12.   Top with pesto sauce and serve.

Did you know?

Gnocchi is Italian for dumplings. Gnocchi with tomato sauce is known as strangolapreti or strangoloprevete, meaning priest stranglers, because a local priest liked them so much, and ate them so fast, that he choked on them.

DAY 21

Meal	Recipe	Calories
Breakfast	Crust less Spinach Quiche	561
Lunch	Creamy Mustard Greens and Spinach Soup	725
Dinner	Roasted Vegetables Salad	722

Crust less Spinach Quiche

INGREDIENTS	Fats	Proteins	Carbs
1 cup spinach	0.12 g	0.86 g	1.09 g
1 egg	4.18 g	5.53 g	0.32 g

1/2 cup cheddar, shredded	19.11 g	13.58 g	0.75 g
1/4 cup blue cheese, crumbled	9.71 g	7.23 g	0.79 g
1 tbsp. white onion, chopped	0.01 g	0.06 g	0.6 g
1/2 tbsp. garlic, chopped	0.02 g	0.27 g	1.42 g
1 tbsp. butter	11.52 g	0.12 g	0.01 g
1/4 cup whole milk	1.99 g	1.92 g	2.92 g

Nutrition Facts

Amount per 252 g
1 serving (8.9 oz)

Calories 567
From fat 416

	Amount	% Daily Value*	Amount	% Daily Value*
Total Fat	46.7g	72%	Total Carbohydrates 8g	3%
Saturated	27.1g	135%	Dietary Fiber 1g	3%
Trans Fat	1.1g		Sugars 4g	
Cholesterol	283mg	94%	Protein 30g	59%
Sodium	867mg	36%		
Calcium 70% • Iron 11%			Vitamin A 86% • Vitamin C 17%	

* Percent Daily Values are based on 2000 calorie diet. Your Daily Values may be higher or lower depending on your calorie needs.

Directions:

1.   Preheat the oven to 375 F.

2.   Grease a muffin pan with butter.

3.   In a large bowl, combine the egg, spinach, cheddar, blue cheese, white onion, garlic, and milk. Whisk together until completely mixed.

4.   Pour the mixture into the muffin pan.

5.   Bake for about 30 minutes, or unit the edges start to turn brown.

6.   Remove from the oven and allow to cool before serving.

Did you know?

Blue cheeses are semisoft cheeses that are marbled with delicate veins of blue-green mold. The blue mold in these cheeses is due to mold spores from Penicillium roqueforti or Penicillium glaucum, etc.

Creamy Mustard Greens and

Spinach Soup

INGREDIENTS	Fats	Proteins	Carbs
3 tbsp. olive oil	40.5 g	0 g	0 g
1/2 tsp cumin	0.24 g	0.2 g	0.49 g
1 tsp coriander	0 g	0.01 g	0.01 g
1/4 tsp turmeric	0.03 g	0.08 g	0.54 g
1/2 tsp paprika	0.15 g	0.17 g	0.65 g
1/2 tbsp. white onion, chopped	0.01 g	0.06 g	0.47 g
1/2 tbsp. ginger, chopped	0.02 g	0.05 g	0.53 g
1/4 tbsp. garlic, chopped	0.01 g	0.13 g	0.69 g

1/2 tbsp. jalapeno, chopped	0.01 g	0.04 g	0.26 g
1/2 cup mustard greens	0.12 g	0.8 g	1.31 g
1 cup spinach	0.12 g	0.86 g	1.09 g
3/4 cup coconut milk	36.15 g	3.42 g	4.76 g

Nutrition Facts

Amount per 286 g
1 serving (10.1 oz)

Calories 725
From fat 667

Amount	% Daily Value*	Amount	% Daily Value*
Total Fat 77.4g	119%	Total Carbohydrates 11g	4%
Saturated 37.7g	189%	Dietary Fiber 3g	10%
Trans Fat 0g		Sugars 1g	
Cholesterol 0mg	0%	Protein 6g	12%
Sodium 56mg	2%		
Calcium 11% • Iron 48%		Vitamin A 87% • Vitamin C 60%	

* Percent Daily Values are based on 2000 calorie diet. Your Daily Values may be higher or lower depending on your calorie needs.

Directions:

1.   In a medium-sized pot, heat 1 tbsp. of olive oil over medium heat.

2.   Add the cumin, coriander, and turmeric. Let the spices brown for 1 to 2 minutes.

3.   Add the white onion and sauté until translucent. Add the ginger, garlic, and jalapeno. Stir while cooking for an additional 1 to 2 minutes.

4.   Add the spinach and mustard green. Sauté until the leaves have wilted, which should take 8 to 10 minutes.

5.   Add the coconut milk and stir. Cook for an additional minute.

6.   Transfer the contents of the pot into a blender. Blend until smooth.

7.   Transfer the soup into a bowl.

8.   In a frying pan, heat some olive oil and add in the remaining garlic and paprika. Stir for a few minutes.

9.   Drizzle the seasoned olive oil over the soup. Serve while hot.

Did you know?

Leaves of coriander (also known as cilantro in North and South America) have fresh, grassy, lemony taste, while seed have sweet, nutty, warm and orange-like flavor.

Roasted Vegetables Salad

INGREDIENTS	Fats	Proteins	Carbs
1/2 tbsp. poppy seeds	1.83 g	0.79 g	1.24 g
1/2 tbsp. sesame seeds	2.45 g	0.82 g	0.47 g

1/4 tsp red onion, chopped	0 g	0.03 g	0.23 g
1/2 tsp garlic, chopped	0.01 g	0.09 g	0.46 g
3/4 cup cheddar, shredded	28.68 g	20.39 g	1.13 g
1/2 cup bell pepper, chopped	0.13 g	0.64 g	3.46 g
1/4 cup white mushrooms, chopped	0.08 g	0.74 g	0.78 g
1 cup arugula	0.13 g	0.52 g	0.73 g
1 tbsp. avocado oil	14 g	0 g	0 g
1 tbsp. olive oil	13.5 g	0 g	0 g

Nutrition Facts

Amount per 243 g
1 serving (8.6 oz)

Calories 664
From fat 540

Amount	% Daily Value*	Amount	% Daily Value*
Total Fat 60.8g	94%	Total Carbohydrates 9g	3%
Saturated 20.5g	103%	Dietary Fiber 3g	13%
Trans Fat 1g		Sugars 3g	
Cholesterol 86mg	29%	Protein 24g	48%
Sodium 559mg	23%		
Calcium 68% • Iron 9%		Vitamin A 32% • Vitamin C 107%	

* Percent Daily Values are based on 2000 calorie diet. Your Daily Values may be higher or lower depending on your calorie needs.

Directions:

1.   In a small bowl, toss together the bell pepper, white mushroom, and olive oil. Ensure that all pieces are covered in oil.

2.   In a small frying pan over high heat, char the bell pepper and mushrooms. Do this just until the skin of the pepper starts to turn black and the pepper becomes tender.

3.   Remove from the heat and set aside.

4.   To the same pan, toast the poppy seeds and sesame seeds. Cook for 1 to 2 minutes, or until fragrant.

5.   In a large bowl combine the arugula, garlic, and onions.

6.   Add the cooked mushrooms and bell peppers.

7.   Sprinkle with the toasted poppy seeds and sesame seeds. Top with cheddar cheese.

8.   Drizzle with avocado oil. Season with salt and pepper, if desired.

9.   Toss the salad and serve

Did you know?

Poppy seeds are excellent source B-complex vita metabolism, especially fat and carbohydrates inside the human body. mins such as thiamin, pantothenic acid, pyridoxine, riboflavin, niacin, and folic acid. Many of these vitamins functions as co-factors in the substrate

DAY 22

Meal	Recipe	Calories
Breakfast	Keto Buttermilk Pancakes	774
Lunch	Four Cheese Pesto Zoodles	787
Dinner	Keto Summer Salad	327

Keto Buttermilk Pancakes

Nutrition Facts

Amount per 351 g
1 serving (12.4 oz)

Calories 774
From fat 604

Amount	% Daily Value*	Amount	% Daily Value*
Total Fat 69.3g	107%	Total Carbohydrates 8g	3%
Saturated 44.8g	224%	Dietary Fiber 1g	4%
Trans Fat 0.6g		Sugars 1g	
Cholesterol 934mg	311%	Protein 33g	66%
Sodium 450mg	19%		
Calcium 22% • Iron 38%		Vitamin A 33% • Vitamin C 1%	

* Percent Daily Values are based on 2000 calorie diet. Your Daily Values may be higher or lower depending on your calorie needs.

INGREDIENTS	Fats	Proteins	Carbs
1 egg	23.11 g	30.52 g	1.75 g
1/4 cup coconut milk	12.05 g	1.14 g	1.59 g
1/2 tbsp. apple cider vinegar	0 g	0 g	0.07 g
1 1/2 tbsp. coconut flour	8.29 g	0.64 g	2.58 g
1/4 tbsp. flaxseed, ground	0.76 g	0.33 g	0.52 g
1/4 tsp cinnamon, ground	0.01 g	0.03 g	0.56 g
1/4 tsp baking powder	0.01 g	0 g	0.61 g
1 tbsp. butter, melted	11.52 g	0.12 g	0.01 g
1 tbsp. coconut oil	13.6 g	0 g	0 g

Directions:

1.   Add the apple cider vinegar to the coconut milk and set aside.

2.   In a separate bowl, combine the dry ingredients: coconut flour, flaxseed, cinnamon, and baking powder. Add a pinch of salt.

3.   Whisk the egg until frothy. Combine the whisked egg with the coconut milk and melted butter.

4.   Fold in the dry ingredients with the wet ingredients. Mix only until there are no more lumps. Do not overmix.
5.   Brush a small frying pan with coconut oil and place over medium heat.

6.   Place on spoonful of the pancake batter into the frying pan. Cook until bubbles break into the surface. Flip and cook on the other side for a few more seconds.

7.   Repeat until all the batter has been used.

8.   Serve while hot.

Did you know?
Coconut Water Can Be Used as a Substitute for Blood Plasma

Four Cheese Pesto Zoodles

INGREDIENTS	Fats	Proteins	Carbs
1 large zucchini	0.06 g	0.43 g	0.5 g
1/2 cup pesto sauce	68.05 g	12.1 g	4.95 g
1/8 tsp nutmeg	0.11 g	0.02 g	0.15 g
1/2 tbsp. parmesan, grated	0.7 g	0.71 g	0.35 g
1/8 cup mozzarella, shredded	3.26 g	3.24 g	0.32 g
1/8 cup feta, crumbled	4.15 g	2.77 g	0.8 g
1/2 tbsp. blue cheese	1.15 g	0.86 g	0.09 g

Nutrition Facts

Amount per 173 g
1 serving (6.1 oz)

Calories 787
From fat 676

Amount	% Daily Value*	Amount	% Daily Value*
Total Fat 77.5g	119%	Total Carbohydrates 7g	2%
Saturated 17.5g	87%	Dietary Fiber 1g	6%
Trans Fat 0g		Sugars 2g	
Cholesterol 54mg	18%	Protein 20g	40%
Sodium 1478mg	62%		
Calcium 51% • Iron 15%		Vitamin A 33% • Vitamin C 17%	

* Percent Daily Values are based on 2000 calorie diet. Your Daily Values may be higher or lower depending on your calorie needs.

Directions:

1.   Using a spiralizer, cut the zucchini into strands.

2.   With a clean kitchen towel, squeeze out as much moisture as you can from the zucchini noodles. Set aside.

3.   In a microwave-safe bowl, combine the parmesan, mozzarella, feta and blue cheese. Microwave on high for 20 to 30 seconds, or just until the cheese has melted.

4.   In a large bowl, combine the zucchini noodles, pesto sauce, and the melted cheese. Season with salt and pepper, if desired. Toss together until thoroughly mixed.

5.   Serve immediately.

Did you know?

The active principles in nutmeg have many therapeutic applications in many traditional medicines as anti-fungal, anti-depressant, aphrodisiac, digestive, and carminative functions.

Keto Summer Salad

INGREDIENTS	Fats	Proteins	Carbs
1 cup romaine lettuce	0.14 g	0.58 g	1.55 g
1/2 cup arugula	0.07 g	0.26 g	0.37 g
1/4 cup celery, chopped	5.35 g	0.73 g	3.11 g
1/4 cup avocado, sliced	0.04 g	0.17 g	0.75 g
1/4 cup cucumber, chopped	0.05 g	0.18 g	0.64 g
1 tbsp. olive oil	13.5 g	0 g	0 g
1/2 tbsp. balsamic vinegar	0 g	0.04 g	1.36 g
1 tbsp. avocado oil	14 g	0 g	0 g

Nutrition Facts	Amount	% Daily Value*	Amount	% Daily Value*
	Total Fat 33.2g	51%	Total Carbohydrates 8g	3%
Amount per 184 g	Saturated 4.3g	22%	Dietary Fiber 4g	17%
1 serving (6.5 oz)	Trans Fat 0g		Sugars 3g	.
	Cholesterol 0mg	0%	Protein 2g	4%
Calories 327	Sodium 32mg	1%		
From fat 290	Calcium 5% • Iron 6%		Vitamin A 90% • Vitamin C 15%	

* Percent Daily Values are based on 2000 calorie diet. Your Daily Values may be higher or lower depending on your calorie needs.

Directions:

1. In a large bowl, combine the lettuce, arugula, celery, cucumber, and avocado.

2.   Drizzle with olive oil, balsamic vinegar, and avocado oil. Season with salt and pepper, if desired.

3.   Toss to mix thoroughly. Serve immediately.

Did you know?

you eat cucumber slices before going to bed, you will wake up feeling fresh and headache free!

DAY 23

Meal	Recipe	Calories
Breakfast	Eggs with Mayonnaise and Roasted Vegetables	429
Lunch	Collard Greens in Coconut Stew	687
Dinner	Zoodles Alfredo	696

Eggs with Mayonnaise and Roasted Vegetables

INGREDIENTS	Fats	Proteins	Carbs
2 eggs	8.37 g	11.05 g	0.63 g
1 tbsp. mayonnaise	10.33 g	0.13 g	0.08 g
3 spears asparagus	0.06 g	1.06 g	1.86 g
1 1/2 tbsp. olive oil	20.3 g	0 g	0 g
1 cup eggplant, diced	0.15 g	0.8 g	4.82 g

Nutrition Facts	Amount	% Daily Value*	Amount	% Daily Value*
Amount per 252 g	**Total Fat** 39.2g	60%	**Total Carbohydrates** 7g	2%
1 serving (8.9 oz)	Saturated 7.2g	36%	Dietary Fiber 4g	14%
	Trans Fat 0.1g		Sugars 4g	
Calories 429	**Cholesterol** 333mg	111%	**Protein** 13g	26%
From fat 350	**Sodium** 216mg	9%		
	Calcium 7% • **Iron** 16%		**Vitamin A** 17% • **Vitamin C** 8%	

* Percent Daily Values are based on 2000 calorie diet. Your Daily Values may be higher or lower depending on your calorie needs.

Directions:

1.   Preheat the oven to 425 F.

2.   Boil the eggs. Cooking time may vary according to your desired doneness.

3.   On a small baking tray, toss the asparagus and eggplant in olive oil. Season with salt and pepper.

4.   Bake for 18 to 20 minutes, or until the asparagus is tender.

5.   Serve the boiled eggs topped with mayonnaise and a side of the roasted vegetables!

Did you know?
An egg contains 2/3 of your recommended cholesterol intake, but it turns out this isn't a big deal. Studies show that regular egg consumption does not increase risk of heart disease.

Collard Greens in Coconut Stew

INGREDIENTS	Fats	Proteins	Carbs
1 cup collard greens, chopped	0.22 g	1.09 g	1.95 g
1/2 cup coconut milk	24.1 g	2.28 g	3.18 g
1/2 cup vegetable broth	0 g	0 g	1.5 g
1/2 tbsp. lime juice	0.01 g	0.03 g	0.64 g
1 tbsp. tahini	8.06 g	2.55 g	3.18 g
3 tbsp. coconut oil	40.8 g	0 g	0 g
1/2 tbsp. ginger, grated	0.02 g	0.05 g	0.53 g
1/2 tbsp. garlic	0.01 g	0.09 g	0.46 g

Nutrition Facts

Amount per 334 g
1 serving (11.8 oz)

Calories 687
From fat 623

Amount	% Daily Value*	Amount	% Daily Value*
Total Fat 73.2g	113%	Total Carbohydrates 11g	4%
Saturated 57.8g	289%	Dietary Fiber 3g	12%
Trans Fat 0.1g		Sugars 1g	
Cholesterol 0mg	0%	Protein 6g	12%
Sodium 509mg	21%		
Calcium 17% • Iron 30%		Vitamin A 41% • Vitamin C 28%	

* Percent Daily Values are based on 2000 calorie diet. Your Daily Values may be higher or lower depending on your calorie needs.

Directions:

1.   Melt the coconut oil over medium heat. Add the ginger and garlic and sauté for 5 minutes.

2.   Add the collard greens and stir for 1 to 2 minutes, or until they have started to wilt.

3.   Add the vegetable broth, coconut milk, and lime juice. Allow to boil and lower the heat to a simmer. Add the tahini and stir the soup.

4.   Cook for an additional 15 minutes. Season with salt and pepper, if desired.

5.   Serve while hot.

Did you know?

Collard greens is rich source of dietary fibers, vitamin B9, C, A, K and minerals such as iron, calcium, copper, manganese and selenium. 100 g of collard greens contains only 30 calories.

Zoodles Alfredo

INGREDIENTS	Fats	Proteins	Carbs
1 medium zucchini	0.04 g	0.3 g	0.34 g
2tbsp.butter	23.04 g	0.24 g	0.02 g
1 tbsp. cream cheese	4.96 g	0.86 g	0.59 g
1 tbsp. sour cream	1.27 g	0.42 g	0.85 g
1 cup heavy cream	44.4 g	2.46 g	3.35 g
1/2 tbsp. parmesan, grated	0.7 g	0.71 g	0.35 g

Nutrition Facts

Amount per 188 g
1 serving (6.6 oz)

Calories 696
From fat 654

Amount	% Daily Value*	Amount	% Daily Value*
Total Fat 74.4g	114%	**Total Carbohydrates** 6g	2%
Saturated 46.2g	231%	Dietary Fiber 0g	0%
Trans Fat 1g		Sugars 4g	
Cholesterol 248mg	83%	**Protein** 5g	10%
Sodium 157mg	7%		
Calcium 14% • **Iron** 1%		**Vitamin A** 56% • **Vitamin C** 8%	

* Percent Daily Values are based on 2000 calorie diet. Your Daily Values may be higher or lower depending on your calorie needs.

Directions:

1.   Using a spiralizer, cut the zucchini into strands.

2.   With a clean kitchen towel, squeeze out as much moisture as you can from the zucchini noodles. Set aside.

3.   In a small saucepan, melt the butter over medium heat.

4.   Add the heavy cream, cream cheese, parmesan, and sour cream. Simmer until all the cheese has melted.

5.   Pour the cheese sauce over the zucchini noodles. Season with salt and pepper, if desired. Toss to mix thoroughly.

Did you know?

Sour Cream (cultured sour cream) is the product resulting from adding lactic acid bacteria to pasteurized cream at least 18% milk fat.

191

DAY 24

Meal	Recipe	Calories
Breakfast	Mini Eggplant Pizzas	418
Lunch	Sesame Tofu Salad	668
Dinner	Keto Falafel with Tahini Sauce	687

Mini Eggplant Pizzas

INGREDIENTS	Fats	Proteins	Carbs
1/4 eggplant	0.12 g	0.67 g	4.03 g
1 egg	4.18 g	5.53 g	0.32 g
2 tbsp. parmesan, grated	2.78 g	2.84 g	1.39 g
2 tbsp. mozzarella, crumbled	3.58 g	3.55 g	0.35 g
1 tbsp. olives, chopped	0.9 g	0.07 g	0.53 g
2 tbsp. olive oil	27 g	0 g	0 g

Nutrition Facts

Amount per 174 g
1 serving (6.1 oz)

Calories 418
From fat 341

Amount	% Daily Value*	Amount	% Daily Value*
Total Fat 38.6g	59%	Total Carbohydrates 7g	2%
Saturated 8.9g	44%	Dietary Fiber 2g	9%
Trans Fat 0.1g		Sugars 3g	
Cholesterol 185mg	62%	Protein 13g	25%
Sodium 407mg	17%		
Calcium 21% • Iron 8%		Vitamin A 10% • Vitamin C 3%	

* Percent Daily Values are based on 2000 calorie diet. Your Daily Values may be higher or lower depending on your calorie needs.

Directions:

1.   Preheat the oven to 425 C.

2.   Slice the eggplant into 1/2-inch thick rounds.

3.   In a small bowl, combine the egg, olive oil, olives parmesan, and mozzarella. Whisk together until thoroughly combined.

4.   Top the eggplant slices with the egg mixture.

5.   Arrange the eggplant slices on a baking tray, taking care not to have them touch each other.

6.   Bake for 18 to 20 minutes, or until the toppings have turned golden brown.

7.   Serve while hot.

Did you know?
There are more than 2000 varieties of cheese available worldwide, mozzarella is the favourite around the globe, and the most consumed. That's quite impressive!

Sesame Tofu Salad

INGREDIENTS	Fats	Proteins	Carbs
1 cup collard greens, chopped	0.22 g	1.09 g	1.95 g
1/2 tbsp. tahini	4.03 g	1.28 g	1.59 g
1/4 cup firm tofu, diced	5.49 g	9.94 g	2.69 g
1 tbsp. sesame seeds	4.9 g	1.64 g	0.94 g
3 tbsp. sesame oil	40.8 g	0 g	0 g
1/2 tbsp. soy sauce	0.05 g	0.65 g	0.39 g
2 tbsp. walnuts, chopped	10.43 g	2.44 g	2.19 g

Nutrition Facts

Amount per 179 g
1 serving (6.3 oz)

Calories 668
From fat 571

Amount	% Daily Value*	Amount	% Daily Value*
Total Fat 65.9g	101%	Total Carbohydrates 10g	3%
Saturated 8.9g	44%	Dietary Fiber 6g	23%
Trans Fat 0g		Sugars 1g	
Cholesterol 0mg	0%	Protein 17g	34%
Sodium 467mg	19%		
Calcium 57% • Iron 20%		Vitamin A 39% • Vitamin C 22%	

* Percent Daily Values are based on 2000 calorie diet. Your Daily Values may be higher or lower depending on your calorie needs.

Directions:

1.   In a bowl, combine the 2 tbsp. sesame oil, soy sauce, and tahini.

2.   Mix in the tofu cubes. Place the marinade mixture in an airtight container and marinate in the refrigerator for at least 2 hours.

3.   In a small frying pan, toast the walnuts over low heat until fragrant, which should take 2 to 3 minutes.

4.   After the tofu cubes have been marinated, arrange them on a parchment-lined baking tray.

5.   Bake in a 425 F preheated oven for 24 to 25 minutes, or until the tofu has turned golden brown with a firm texture.

6.   In a large bowl, combine the collard greens, cooked tofu, and walnuts. Toss and serve.

Did you know?

Sesame doesn't contain gluten, it's perfect for celiacs and those who would like to avoid eating gluten.

Keto Falafel with Tahini Sauce

INGREDIENTS	Fats	Proteins	Carbs
1/4 cup cauliflower, chopped	0.08 g	0.51 g	1.33 g
2 tbsp. almonds, slivered	7.99 g	3.38 g	3.45 g
1/4 tbsp. cumin	0.33 g	0.27 g	0.66 g
1/4 tbsp. coriander	0 g	0.01 g	0.01 g
1/2 tsp garlic, chopped	0.01 g	0.09 g	0.46 g
1/2 tbsp. parsley, chopped	0.02 g	0.06 g	0.12 g
1 egg	4.18 g	5.53 g	0.32 g
1/2 tbsp. coconut flour	2.76 g	0.21 g	0.86 g
1/2 tbsp. tahini	4.03 g	1.28 g	1.59 g
1/2 tbsp. lemon juice	0.02 g	0.03 g	0.52 g
2 tbsp. olive oil	27 g	0 g	0 g
2 tbsp. butter	23.04 g	0.24 g	0.02 g

Nutrition Facts

Amount per 166 g
1 serving (5.9 oz)

Calories 687
From fat 606

Amount	% Daily Value*	Amount	% Daily Value*
Total Fat 69.5g	107%	Total Carbohydrates 9g	3%
Saturated 23.4g	117%	Dietary Fiber 4g	14%
Trans Fat 1g		Sugars 2g	
Cholesterol 225mg	75%	Protein 12g	23%
Sodium 88mg	4%		
Calcium 13% • Iron 20%		Vitamin A 23% • Vitamin C 32%	

* Percent Daily Values are based on 2000 calorie diet. Your Daily Values may be higher or lower depending on your calorie needs.

Directions:

1.   In a food processor, combine the cauliflower and almonds. Pulse until a fine powder-like consistency is achieved.

2.   Add the cumin, coriander, garlic, egg, coconut flour, butter, and parsley. Pulse again until everything has been well incorporated.

3.   Form the batter into 1/2-inch thick patties.

4.   Heat the olive oil in a small frying pan over medium heat.

5.   Cook the patties on one side 4 to 5 minutes, ensuring that it has turned a golden brown color. Flip to the other side and cook for another 4 to 5 minutes.

6.   Repeat until all the batter and the patties have been cooked.

7.   For the tahini sauce, combine the tahini and lemon juice and mix until well-incorporated.

8.   Serve the falafels with the tahini sauce on the side.

Did you know?

Olive oil has a higher proportion of monounsaturated fats than animal fat, which is often high in saturated fat. Studies have indicated that if you replace saturated fats with monounsaturated fats, you can lower your risk of coronary heart disease.

DAY 25

Meal	Recipe	Calories
Breakfast	Pumpkin Breakfast Porridge	629
Lunch	Mediterranean Cauliflower Pizza	641
Dinner	Roasted Asparagus with Buttermilk Dressing	559

Pumpkin Breakfast Porridge

INGREDIENTS	Fats	Proteins	Carbs
1 tbsp. peanut flour	0.83 g	1.28 g	1.19 g
1/2 tbsp. flaxseed, ground	1.48 g	0.64 g	1.01 g
1/4 tsp pumpkin spice	0.05 g	0.02 g	0.28 g
1 egg	4.18 g	5.53 g	0.32 g
1/4 tsp vanilla extract	0 g	0 g	0.14 g
2 tbsp. canned pumpkin	0.09 g	0.34 g	2.48 g
1 cup heavy cream	44.4 g	2.46 g	3.35 g
1 tbsp. butter	11.52 g	0.12 g	0.01 g

Nutrition Facts

Amount per 218 g
1 serving (7.7 oz)

Calories 629
From fat 550

	Amount	% Daily Value*	Amount	% Daily Value*
	Total Fat 62.6g	96%	Total Carbohydrates 9g	3%
	Saturated 36.6g	183%	Dietary Fiber 3g	10%
	Trans Fat 0.5g		Sugars 5g	
	Cholesterol 359mg	120%	Protein 10g	21%
	Sodium 202mg	8%		
	Calcium 13% • Iron 9%		Vitamin A 142% • Vitamin C 4%	

* Percent Daily Values are based on 2000 calorie diet. Your Daily Values may be higher or lower depending on your calorie needs.

Directions:

1.   In a small pot, combine the peanut flour, flaxseed, pumpkin spice, heavy cream, canned pumpkin, and butter.

2.   Boil the mixture over high heat, then lower the heat to a simmer.

3.   Whisk the egg in a small bowl. Slowly add the whisked egg into the soup while continuously stirring. Continue cooking the soup while stirring until it thickens up.

4.   Add the vanilla extract and flaxseed. Cook for another 5 minutes.

5.   Ladle the soup into a bowl. Serve while hot.

Did you know?

Flaxseed oil can heal inflamed skin areas in cases of acne, rosacea, and eczema. The topical application of this oil heals sunburns effectively.

Mediterranean Cauliflower Pizza

INGREDIENTS	Fats	Proteins	Carbs
1/4 cup cauliflower, chopped	0.08 g	0.51 g	1.33 g
2 tbsp. parmesan, grated	2.78 g	2.84 g	1.39 g
1/2 tbsp. almond paste	1.11 g	0.36 g	1.91 g
1/4 tsp garlic powder	0.01 g	0.13 g	0.58 g
1 egg	4.18 g	5.53 g	0.32 g
1/4 tsp dried oregano	0.01 g	0.03 g	0.21 g

1//2 tbsp. tomato paste	0.04 g	0.35 g	1.51 g
1 tbsp. olives, sliced	0.9 g	0.07 g	0.53 g
1 tbsp. basil	0.02 g	0.09 g	0.07 g
2 tbsp. olive oil	27 g	0 g	0 g
3/4 cup mozzarella	18.77 g	18.62 g	1.84 g

Nutrition Facts

Amount per 216 g
1 serving (7.6 oz)

Calories 641
From fat 484

Amount	% Daily Value*	Amount	% Daily Value*
Total Fat 54.9g	84%	Total Carbohydrates 10g	3%
Saturated 18g	90%	Dietary Fiber 2g	6%
Trans Fat 0.1g		Sugars 4g	
Cholesterol 239mg	80%	Protein 29g	57%
Sodium 846mg	35%		
Calcium 57% • Iron 13%		Vitamin A 24% • Vitamin C 26%	

* Percent Daily Values are based on 2000 calorie diet. Your Daily Values may be higher or lower depending on your calorie needs.

Directions:

1.   Preheat the oven to 450 F.

2.   Place the cauliflower in a food processor and pulse until a rice-like texture is achieved.

3.   Place the riced cauliflower in a microwave safe bowl. Microwave on high for about 7 to 8 minutes.

4.   In a small bowl, combine the cooked cauliflower, parmesan, almond paste, garlic powder, and egg. Season with salt. Mix thoroughly until a homogenous batter is formed.

5.   Place the batter on a baking tray lined with parchment paper. Spread the batter to form the shape of a pizza crust.

6.　　Bake the pizza crust in the oven for 14 to 15 minutes.

7.　　Remove the crust from the oven and assemble the pizza.

8.　　Spread the tomato paste evenly over the pizza. Tops with sliced olives and mozzarella.

9.　　Put the pizza back on the oven and bake for an addition 2 or 3 minutes, just until the cheese has melted.

10.　　Serve hot.

Did you know?
There are more than 450 varieties of garlic.

Roasted Asparagus with Buttermilk Dressing

INGREDIENTS	Fats	Proteins	Carbs
1/2 tsp. garlic, crushed	0.01 g	0.09 g	0.46 g
2 tbsp. buttermilk	1.01 g	0.98 g	1.49 g
1 tbsp. distilled vinegar	0 g	0 g	0.01 g
2 1/2 tbsp. olive oil	33.8 g	0 g	0 g

4 spears asparagus	0.08 g	1.41 g	2.48 g
1 tbsp. cilantro, chopped	0.01 g	0.02 g	0.04 g
1/2 tbsp. sunflower seeds	2.26 g	0.91 g	0.88 g
1/2 cup feta, crumbled	15.96 g	10.66 g	3.07 g

Nutrition Facts

Amount per 225 g
5 servings (7.9 oz)

Calories 559
From fat 468

Amount	% Daily Value*	Amount	% Daily Value*
Total Fat 53.1g	82%	Total Carbohydrates 8g	3%
Saturated 16.7g	83%	Dietary Fiber 2g	7%
Trans Fat 0g		Sugars 6g	
Cholesterol 70mg	23%	Protein 14g	28%
Sodium 723mg	30%		
Calcium 43% • Iron 13%		Vitamin A 18% • Vitamin C 7%	

* Percent Daily Values are based on 2000 calorie diet. Your Daily Values may be higher or lower depending on your calorie needs.

Directions:

1.   Preheat the oven to 425 F.

2.   On a baking tray, toss the asparagus with 2 tbsp olive oil, garlic, and sunflower seeds.

3.   Bake the asparagus in the oven for 19 to 20 minutes, or until the asparagus is tender.

4.   Remove the asparagus from the oven and place on a small bowl.

5.   Drizzle the asparagus with the buttermilk, vinegar, and the remaining olive oil. Add the cilantro and feta. Toss the salad completely before serving.

Did you know?

You can use full strength white distilled vinegar to kill grass on sidewalks and driveways.

DAY 26

Meal	Recipe	Calories
Breakfast	Grain-Free Overnight Oats	586
Lunch	Cucumber Salad with Wasabi Dressing	657
Dinner	Roasted Cauliflower and Tofu	658

Grain-Free Overnight Oats

INGREDIENTS	Fats	Proteins	Carbs
1/2 cup coconut milk	24.1 g	2.28 g	3.18 g
1/4 tbsp. chia seeds	0.61 g	0.33 g	0.84 g
1 tbsp. desiccated coconut	0.03 g	0.11 g	0.56 g
1 tsp sunflower seeds	1.49 g	0.6 g	0.58 g
1/2 tsp vanilla extract	0 g	0 g	0.27 g
1 tbsp. almonds, slivered	3.99 g	1.69 g	1.72 g
2 tbsp. coconut oil	27.2 g	0 g	0 g

1 1/2 tbsp. protein powder	1.44 g	6 g	2.64 g

Directions:

1. In a blender, combine the coconut milk, protein powder, coconut oil, and vanilla extract. Blend until smooth.

2. Transfer the contents of the blender into an airtight container. Add the chia seeds, desiccated coconut, and sunflower seeds. Mix thoroughly and cover. Leave overnight.

3. The following day, add the slivered almonds before serving.

Did you know?

The word chia originated from the Aztecs word for oily, chian.

Cucumber Salad With Wasabi Dressing

INGREDIENTS	Fats	Proteins	Carbs
1/4 cup cucumber, sliced	0.08 g	0.3 g	1.09 g
3/4 cup romaine lettuce, shredded	0.11 g	0.43 g	1.16 g
1 tsp sesame seeds	1.65 g	0.55 g	0.32 g
2 tbsp. avocado, diced	2.35 g	0.32 g	1.36 g
1 tbsp. green onion, sliced	0.03 g	0.06 g	0.34 g
1 tbsp. lime juice	0.01 g	0.06 g	1.27 g
1/2 tbsp. wasabi powder	0.03 g	0.19 g	0.94 g
2 tbsp. avocado oil	28 g	0 g	0 g
2 tsp vinegar	0 g	0 g	0.09 g
2 tbsp. olive oil	27 g	0 g	0 g
8 tbsp. walnuts	10.43 g	2.44 g	2.19 g

Nutrition Facts	Amount	% Daily Value*	Amount	% Daily Value*
Amount per 210 g	Total Fat 69.7g	107%	Total Carbohydrates 9g	3%
1 serving (7.4 oz)	Saturated 8.6g	43%	Dietary Fiber 4g	16%
	Trans Fat 0g		Sugars 2g	
Calories 657	Cholesterol 0mg	0%	Protein 4g	9%
From fat 609	Sodium 9mg	0%		
	Calcium 5% • Iron 8%		Vitamin A 68% • Vitamin C 20%	

* Percent Daily Values are based on 2000 calorie diet. Your Daily Values may be higher or lower depending on your calorie needs.

Directions:

1.   Prepare the dressing by combining the lime juice, wasabi powder, avocado oil, vinegar, and olive oil. Whisk together until well combined.

2.   In a large bowl, combine the sliced cucumber, romaine lettuce, avocado, green onion, walnuts, and sesame seeds.

3.   Drizzle with the dressing and toss to combine. Serve immediately.

Did you know?

Wasabi or Japanese horseradish is a plant of the Brassicaceae family, which includes cabbages, horseradish, and mustard.

Roasted Cauliflower and Tofu

INGREDIENTS	Fats	Proteins	Carbs
1/2 cup cauliflower, sliced	0.15 g	1.03 g	2.66 g
1/4 cup firm tofu, diced	5.49 g	9.94 g	2.69 g
3/4 tbsp. tahini	6.07 g	1.92 g	2.39 g
2 tbsp. olive oil	27 g	0 g	0 g
1/4 tbsp. parmesan, grated	0.36 g	0.37 g	0.18 g
2 tbsp. sesame oil	27.2 g	0 g	0 g
1/2 tbsp. lemon juice	0.02 g	0.03 g	0.52 g

Nutrition Facts

Amount per 191 g
1 serving (6.7 oz)

Calories 658
From fat 581

	Amount	% Daily Value*		Amount	% Daily Value*
Total Fat	66.3g	102%	Total Carbohydrates	8g	3%
Saturated	9.5g	48%	Dietary Fiber	4g	14%
Trans Fat	0g		Sugars	1g	
Cholesterol	1mg	0%	Protein	13g	27%
Sodium	62mg	3%			
Calcium	50% •	Iron 17%	Vitamin A	3% •	Vitamin C 48%

* Percent Daily Values are based on 2000 calorie diet. Your Daily Values may be higher or lower depending on your calorie needs.

Directions:

1.   Preheat the oven to 425 F.

2.   In a baking tray, toss the cauliflower and tofu with the tahini, sesame oil, and olive oil.

3.   Bake in the oven for 24 to 25 minutes, or until the tofu is crispy and the cauliflower is tender.

4.   Remove from the oven and transfer to a bowl.

5.   Spritz the lemon juice over the salad and top with parmesan. Serve while hot.

Did you know?

Tofu is one of the oldest foods in the world: It is said that almost 2000 years ago, tofu was discovered accidentally by a Chinese cook, who curdled soy milk using nigari seaweed. It was then introduced to Japan and called okabe.

DAY 27

Meal	Recipe	Calories
Breakfast	Egg and Avocado Salad	598
Lunch	Jalapeno and Cauliflower Casserole	755
Dinner	Indian Egg Curry	607

Egg and Avocado Salad

INGREDIENTS	Fats	Proteins	Carbs
3 eggs	12.55 g	16.58 g	0.95 g
1/2 cup avocado, diced	11 g	1.5 g	6.4 g
1/2 tbsp. mayonnaise	5.16 g	0.07 g	0.04 g
1/2 tsp mustard	0.08 g	0.09 g	0.15 g
1 tsp lemon juice	0.01 g	0.02 g	0.35 g
1/4 tsp dill	0.02 g	0.07 g	0.14 g
1/4 tsp parsley	0 g	0.01 g	0.02 g
2 tbsp. olive oil	27 g	0 g	0 g

Nutrition Facts

Amount per 215 g
1 serving (7.6 oz)

Calories 572
From fat 452

Amount	% Daily Value*	Amount	% Daily Value*
Total Fat 51.5g	79%	**Total Carbohydrates** 10g	3%
Saturated 16.3g	82%	Dietary Fiber 7g	27%
Trans Fat 0.7g		Sugars 1g	
Cholesterol 221mg	74%	**Protein** 21g	42%
Sodium 434mg	18%		
Calcium 42% • **Iron** 8%		**Vitamin A** 19% • **Vitamin C** 17%	

* Percent Daily Values are based on 2000 calorie diet. Your Daily Values may be higher or lower depending on your calorie needs.

Directions:

1.   Boil the eggs until your desired doneness. After cooking, submerge the eggs immediately into ice water.

2.   Peel the eggs and mash using a fork.

3.   In a separate container, mash the avocados.

4.   Combine the eggs, mashed avocado, mayonnaise, mustard, lemon juice, dill, parsley, and olive oil. Mix thoroughly.

5.   Chill for at least 30 minutes before serving.

Did you know?

Dill can be used in treatment of digestive problems, lack of appetite and jaundice. It reduces flatulence and can be used as a cure for hiccups. Dill stimulates lactation in breastfeeding women and alleviates colic in babies. It can be also used to calm babies and help them fall asleep during teething.

Jalapeno and Cauliflower Casserole

INGREDIENTS	Fats	Proteins	Carbs
1/4 cup cauliflower, chopped	0.08 g	0.51 g	1.33 g
1/2 cup heavy cream	22.2 g	1.23 g	1.67 g
1 tbsp. butter	11.52 g	0.12 g	0.01 g
1/4 cup cheddar, shredded	9.57 g	6.8 g	0.38 g
1/4 cup, jalapeno	0.08 g	0.2 g	1.46 g
1/2 tsp garlic powder	0.01 g	0.26 g	1.16 g
1/4 cup cheddar, shredded	9.57 g	6.8 g	0.38 g
1/4 cup cream cheese	19.86 g	3.44 g	2.36 g

Nutrition Facts

Amount per 240 g
1 serving (8.5 oz)

Calories 755
From fat 645

Amount	% Daily Value*	Amount	% Daily Value*
Total Fat 72.9g	112%	Total Carbohydrates 9g	3%
Saturated 43.3g	217%	Dietary Fiber 1g	5%
Trans Fat 1.1g		Sugars 5g	
Cholesterol 234mg	78%	Protein 19g	39%
Sodium 700mg	29%		
Calcium 49% • Iron 3%		Vitamin A 56% • Vitamin C 67%	

* Percent Daily Values are based on 2000 calorie diet. Your Daily Values may be higher or lower depending on your calorie needs.

Directions:

1.   Preheat the oven to 375 F.

2.   Place the chopped cauliflower in a microwave-safe bowl and microwave on high for 10 minutes. Check to see if

the cauliflower is tender; if not, then microwave for an additional 5 minutes.

3.   Place the cooked cauliflower in a blender and add the heavy cream, 1/4 cup cheddar, jalapeno, butter, and garlic powder. Season with salt and pepper, if desired. Blend until smooth.

4.   Transfer the contents of the blender to an oven-safe dish. Spread the cream cheese over the top, and sprinkle with the remaining cheddar.

5.   Bake the cauliflower casserole in the oven for 20 minutes, or until the cheese on top has melted and browned.

6.   Allow to cool for a few minutes before serving.

Did you know?
The psychological term for fear of garlic is Alliumphobia.

Indian Egg Curry

INGREDIENTS	Fats	Proteins	Carbs
1 egg	4.18 g	5.53 g	0.32 g
1/4 cup snap beans	0.18 g	0.43 g	1.65 g
1/2 tsp green onion, chopped	0 g	0.01 g	0.06 g
1/4 tsp garlic, chopped	0 g	0.04 g	0.23 g
1/4 tsp turmeric	0.03 g	0.08 g	0.54 g
1/2 tsp ginger, grated	0.01 g	0.02 g	0.18 g
1/2 tsp cumin	0.24 g	0.2 g	0.49 g
1/2 tsp coriander	0 g	0g	0.01 g
1/2 tbsp. tomato paste	0.04 g	0.35 g	1.51 g
1/2 cup coconut milk	24.1 g	2.28 g	3.18 g
1/2 tbsp. cilantro	0 g	0.01 g	0.02 g
1/2 tbsp. lime juice	0.01 g	0.03 g	0.64 g
2 tbsp. coconut oil	27.2 g	0 g	0 g

1/2 tbsp. red chili, crushed	0.02 g	0.07 g	0.35 g
1/2 tbsp. sesame oil	6.8 g	0 g	0 g

Nutrition Facts

Amount per 254 g

1 serving (9 oz)

Calories 607

From fat 538

Amount	% Daily Value*	Amount	% Daily Value*
Total Fat 62.8g	97%	Total Carbohydrates 9g	3%
Saturated 47.3g	237%	Dietary Fiber 2g	6%
Trans Fat 0.1g		Sugars 2g	
Cholesterol 164mg	55%	Protein 9g	18%
Sodium 86mg	4%		
Calcium 8% • Iron 36%		Vitamin A 13% • Vitamin C 21%	

* Percent Daily Values are based on 2000 calorie diet. Your Daily Values may be higher or lower depending on your calorie needs.

Directions:

1. Boil the egg in water until the desired doneness. After cooking, submerge the egg immediately in ice water and peel.

2. Melt the coconut oil in a large frying pan over medium heat. Add the sesame oil.

3. To the frying pan, add the garlic, ginger, and red chili. Cook for around 3 minutes.

4. Add the turmeric, cumin, and coriander. Cook for another 3 minutes.

5. Add the tomato paste. Stir and cook for another 3 minutes

6. Add the coconut milk and bring it to a boil. Lower the heat down to a simmer, and simmer for 10 minutes.

7.   Add the boiled egg and the snap beans to the curry. Cook for an additional 8 minutes.

8.   Drizzle the lime juice over the curry and sprinkle with coriander. Serve while hot.

Did you know?
Turmeric paste is a home remedy for sunburn and it is also an ingredient in many commercial sunscreens.

DAY 28

Meal	Recipe	Calories
Breakfast	Creamy Coconut Porridge	602
Lunch	Blue Cheese Coleslaw	531
Dinner	Fried Zucchini Cakes	790

Creamy Coconut Porridge

INGREDIENTS	Fats	Proteins	Carbs
1/2 cup coconut milk	24.1 g	2.28 g	3.18 g
2 tbsp. coconut oil	27.2 g	0 g	0 g
1/2 tbsp. desiccated coconut	2.76 g	0.21 g	0.86 g

1 tsp flaxseed, ground	1.05 g	0.46 g	0.72 g
1/2 tsp chia seeds	1.23 g	0.66 g	1.68 g
1/4 tsp vanilla extract	0 g	0 g	0.14 g
1/4 tsp nutmeg	0.22 g	0.04 g	0.3 g
1 1/2 tbsp. walnuts, chopped	7.83 g	1.83 g	1.65 g

Nutrition Facts

Amount per 164 g
1 serving (5.8 oz)

Calories 602
From fat 546

Amount	% Daily Value*	Amount	% Daily Value*
Total Fat 64.4g	99%	Total Carbohydrates 9g	3%
Saturated 48.5g	242%	Dietary Fiber 3g	12%
Trans Fat 0.1g		Sugars 1g	
Cholesterol 0mg	0%	Protein 5g	11%
Sodium 18mg	1%		
Calcium 7% • Iron 26%		Vitamin A 0% • Vitamin C	2%

* Percent Daily Values are based on 2000 calorie diet. Your Daily Values may be higher or lower depending on your calorie needs.

Directions:

1.   In a saucepan, toast the desiccated coconut over high heat for 4 to 5 minutes. Keep stirring so that the coconut does not burn.

2.   Add the coconut milk and coconut oil bring to a boil.

3.   Add the flaxseed, chia seeds, nutmeg, and vanilla extract. Simmer for an additional 5 minutes.

4.   Transfer to a bowl and top with walnuts. Serve while hot.

Did you know?

The smell of vanilla is known to directly impact the brain and induce calmness.

Blue Cheese Coleslaw

INGREDIENTS	Fats	Proteins	Carbs
1/2 cup red cabbage, shredded	0.06 g	0.5 g	2.58 g
1 tbsp. green onion, chopped	0.03 g	0.06 g	0.34 g
1/2 tbsp. celery, chopped	0.01 g	0.03 g	0.11 g
1/4 cup buttermilk	0.54 g	2.03 g	2.94 g
1/2 cup blue cheese, crumbled	19.4 g	14.45 g	1.58 g
1 1/2 tbsp. butter	17.28 g	0.18 g	0.01 g
1/2 cup green cabbage, shredded	0.04 g	0.45 g	2.03 g
1 tbsp. mayonnaise	10.33 g	0.13 g	0.08 g

Nutrition Facts

Amount per 244 g
1 serving (8.6 oz)

Calories 531
From fat 421

Amount	% Daily Value*	Amount	% Daily Value*
Total Fat 47.7g	73%	Total Carbohydrates 10g	3%
Saturated 25.5g	128%	Dietary Fiber 2g	7%
Trans Fat 0.7g		Sugars 6g	
Cholesterol 105mg	35%	Protein 18g	36%
Sodium 1000mg	42%		
Calcium 47% • Iron 4%		Vitamin A 35% • Vitamin C 57%	

* Percent Daily Values are based on 2000 calorie diet. Your Daily Values may be higher or lower depending on your calorie needs.

Directions:

1.   In a microwave-safe bowl, combine the buttermilk, blue cheese, and butter. Microwave on medium setting for 3 minutes, or until the cheese has melted. Mix the blue cheese mixture immediately after.

2.   In a large bowl, combine the red cabbage, green cabbage, celery, green onion, mayonnaise and the cheese mixture. Season with salt and pepper, if desired.

3.   Toss the coleslaw together.

4.   Chill in the refrigerator for at least 30 minutes before serving.

Did you know?

Cabbage is an excellent source of vitamin K, vitamin C and vitamin B6. It is also a very good source of manganese, dietary fiber, potassium, vitamin B1, folate and copper. Additionally, cabbage is a good source of choline, phosphorus, vitamin B2, magnesium, calcium, selenium, iron, pantothenic acid, protein and niacin.

Fried Zucchini Cakes

INGREDIENTS	Fats	Proteins	Carbs
4 large baby zucchini	0.26 g	1.73 g	1.99 g
1 egg	4.18 g	5.53 g	0.32 g
2 tbsp. desiccated coconut	11.05 g	0.85 g	3.44 g
1/2 tsp garlic powder	0.01 g	0.26 g	1.16 g
1/2 tsp cumin	0.24 g	0.2 g	0.49 g

2 tbsp. butter	23.04 g	0.24 g	0.02 g
1/4 tbsp. sesame seeds	1.22 g	0.41 g	0.23 g
2 tbsp. olive oil	27 g	0 g	0 g
3 tbsp. parmesan, grated	4.18 g	4.26 g	2.09 g
1 tbsp. pesto sauce	8.8 g	1.56 g	0.64 g

Nutrition Facts

Amount per 208 g
1 serving (7.3 oz)

Calories 790
From fat 694

Amount	% Daily Value*	Amount	% Daily Value*
Total Fat 79.4g	122%	Total Carbohydrates 10g	3%
Saturated 33.3g	167%	Dietary Fiber 1g	5%
Trans Fat 1.1g		Sugars 0g	
Cholesterol 218mg	73%	Protein 14g	29%
Sodium 664mg	28%		
Calcium 22% • Iron 18%		Vitamin A 31% • Vitamin C 38%	

* Percent Daily Values are based on 2000 calorie diet. Your Daily Values may be higher or lower depending on your calorie needs.

Directions:

1.   Using a mandolin slicer, slice the zucchini into very fine strips.

2.   Place the zucchini strips on a clean kitchen towel and squeeze as much excess water as possible. Set aside.

3.   In a large bowl, combine the zucchini strips, egg, desiccated coconut, garlic powder, butter, parmesan, cumin, and sesame seeds. Toss together until thoroughly mixed.

4.   Divide the batter into patties of about 3 inches in diameter.

5.   Heat the olive oil in a small frying pan over medium heat.

6. Put the patties into the frying pan. Cook one side for 6 to 7 minutes, or until it turns a golden brown. Flip and cook on the other side for the same length of time.

7. Repeat until all patties have been cooked.

8. Top with pesto sauce. Serve while hot.

Did you know?

Biggest is NOT best. The most flavorful zucchinis are small- to medium-sized and the darker the skin, the richer the nutrients.

DAY 29

Meal	Recipe	Calories
Breakfast	High Protein Green Smoothie	570
Lunch	Simple Greek Salad	675
Dinner	Pesto and Sun-Dried Tomatoes Mug Cake	650

High Protein Green Smoothie

INGREDIENTS	Fats	Proteins	Carbs
1/2 cup spinach	0.06 g	0.43 g	0.54 g

1/4 cup avocado, cubed	5.5 g	0.75 g	3.2 g
2 tbsp. coconut oil	27.2 g	0 g	0 g
1 tsp vanilla extract	0 g	0 g	0.53 g
1/4 cup coconut milk	12.05 g	1.14 g	1.59 g
1/4 cup heavy cream	11.1 g	0.62 g	0.84 g
1 tbsp. protein powder	1.89 g	5.03 g	2.04 g

Nutrition Facts

Amount per 181 g
1 serving (6.4 oz)

Calories 570
From fat 496

Amount	% Daily Value*	Amount	% Daily Value*
Total Fat 57.8g	89%	Total Carbohydrates 9g	3%
Saturated 42.1g	211%	Dietary Fiber 4g	14%
Trans Fat 0g		Sugars 2g	
Cholesterol 43mg	14%	Protein 8g	16%
Sodium 70mg	3%		
Calcium 10% • Iron 19%		Vitamin A 44% • Vitamin C 20%	

* Percent Daily Values are based on 2000 calorie diet. Your Daily Values may be higher or lower depending on your calorie needs.

Directions:

1.   In a blender, combine all the ingredients and add 4 to 5 ice cubes.

2.   Blend until smooth.

3.   Serve and enjoy!

Did you know?

Spinach is best eaten fresh. It loses nutritional properties with each passing day. Although refrigeration slows the deterioration, half of the major nutrients are lost by the eighth day after harvest. (For long term storage, freeze while fresh.)

When fresh, it has crisp leaves. As they deteriorate, the leaves turn limp.

Simple Greek Salad

INGREDIENTS	Fats	Proteins	Carbs
1/2 cup cucumber, diced	0.1 g	0.35 g	1.29 g
3/4 cup feta, crumbled	23.94 g	15.99 g	4.6 g
1 tbsp. dill	0.09 g	0.28 g	0.56 g
3 tbsp. olive oil	40.5 g	0 g	0 g
1/4 cup cherry tomatoes	0.07 g	0.33 g	1.45 g
1/2 cup arugula	0.07 g	0.26 g	0.37 g

Nutrition Facts

Amount per 268 g
1 serving (9.4 oz)

Calories 675
From fat 571

	Amount	% Daily Value*	Amount	% Daily Value*
	Total Fat 64.8g	100%	Total Carbohydrates 8g	3%
	Saturated 22.4g	112%	Dietary Fiber 1g	5%
	Trans Fat 0g		Sugars 7g	
	Cholesterol 100mg	33%	Protein 17g	34%
	Sodium 1043mg	43%		
	Calcium 60% • Iron 10%		Vitamin A 34% • Vitamin C 26%	

* Percent Daily Values are based on 2000 calorie diet. Your Daily Values may be higher or lower depending on your calorie needs.

Directions:

1.   Combine the cucumber, dill, feta, cherry tomatoes, and arugula in a bowl.

2.   Drizzle with olive oil. Season with salt and pepper, if desired.

3.   Toss lightly and serve.

Did you know?

Because the tomato has seeds and grows from a flowering plant botanically it is classed as a fruit not a vegetable.

Pesto and Sun-Dried Tomatoes Mug Cake

INGREDIENTS	Fats	Proteins	Carbs
1 egg	4.18 g	5.53 g	0.32 g
2 tbsp. butter	23.04 g	0.24 g	0.02 g
1/2 tbsp. almond meal	1.11 g	0.36 g	1.91 g
1/2 tsp baking powder	0.01 g	0 g	1.17 g
4 tbsp. pesto sauce	35.2 g	6.26 g	2.56 g
1/2 tbsp. sun dried tomato	0.48 g	0.17 g	0.79 g
1 tbsp. peanut flour	0.02 g	1.98 g	1.32 g

ca

Nutrition Facts

Amount per 146 g
1 serving (5.2 oz)

Calories 650
From fat 561

	Amount	% Daily Value*	Amount	% Daily Value*
Total Fat 64g		99%	Total Carbohydrates 8g	3%
Saturated 22.1g		110%	Dietary Fiber 2g	6%
Trans Fat 0.9g			Sugars 2g	
Cholesterol 235mg		78%	Protein 15g	29%
Sodium 841mg		35%		
Calcium 31% • Iron 13%			Vitamin A 34% • Vitamin C 10%	

* Percent Daily Values are based on 2000 calorie diet. Your Daily Values may be higher or lower depending on your calorie needs.

Directions:

1.   In a mug, combine the egg, almond meal, butter, pesto sauce, sun dried tomato, peanut flour and baking powder. Add a pinch of salt, if desired.

2.   Whisk everything together.

3.   Microwave the mug on the highest setting for exactly 75 seconds.

4.   Invert the mug on top of a plate and tap the bottom of the bug until the cake falls off.

5.   Serve while hot.

Did you know?

There are more than 7500 tomato varieties grown around the world.

DAY 30

Meal	Recipe	Calories
Breakfast	Tofu and Mushroom Scramble	688
Lunch	Broccoli and Cauliflower Salad	685
Dinner	Avocado and Lime Coleslaw	524

Tofu and Mushroom Scramble

INGREDIENTS	Fats	Proteins	Carbs
3 tbsp. olive oil	40.5 g	0 g	0 g
1/4 cup firm tofu, diced	5.49 g	9.94 g	2.69 g
1/2 tbsp. green onion, chopped	0.01 g	0.03 g	0.17 g
1/4 cup white mushrooms, chopped	0.08 g	0.74 g	0.78 g
1/4 cup bell pepper, sliced	0.02 g	0.23 g	1.07 g
1/2 cup spinach	0.06 g	0.43 g	0.54 g
1/2 tsp garlic, chopped	0.01 g	0.09 g	0.46 g
1/2 tsp turmeric	0.05 g	0.15 g	1.01 g
1 egg	4.18 g	5.53 g	0.32 g
3 tbsp. heavy cream	16.65 g	0.92 g	1.26 g

Nutrition Facts	Amount	% Daily Value*	Amount	% Daily Value*
	Total Fat 67.1g	103%	Total Carbohydrates 8g	3%
	Saturated 18.2g	91%	Dietary Fiber 3g	10%
Amount per 249 g	Trans Fat 0g		Sugars 3g	
1 serving (8.8 oz)	Cholesterol 225mg	75%	Protein 18g	36%
Calories 688	Sodium 104mg	4%		
From fat 590	Calcium 51% • Iron 23%		Vitamin A 53% • Vitamin C 56%	

* Percent Daily Values are based on 2000 calorie diet. Your Daily Values may be higher or lower depending on your calorie needs.

Directions:

1.   In a medium-sized frying pan, heat 2 tbsp. olive oil over high heat.

2.   Add the tofu and white mushrooms to the pan. Cook for 9 to 10 minutes while stirring or until the tofu is firm and the mushrooms has turned light brown. Set aside.

3.   In a small bowl, whisk together the egg and heavy cream. Set aside.

4.   In a medium-sized frying pan, heat the remaining olive oil. Pour in the egg mixture.

5.   Add the turmeric, bell pepper, tofu, and mushrooms. Stir the eggs continuously for a minute.

6.   Add the spinach and green onion. Stir and cook for another minute.

7.   Season with salt and pepper, if desired.

8.   Remove from heat and serve immediately.

Did you know?

The scientific name for bell peppers is Capsicum annum

Broccoli and Cauliflower Salad

INGREDIENTS	Fats	Proteins	Carbs
1 1/4 cup broccoli, chopped	0.25 g	1.59 g	1.43 g
1/2 cup cauliflower, chopped	0.15 g	1.03 g	2.66 g
1/2 tbsp. red onion, chopped	0.01 g	0.06 g	0.47 g
1 tbsp. mayonnaise	10.33 g	0.13 g	0.08 g
1/2 tbsp. red wine vinegar	0 g	0 g	0.02 g
1/2 cup Monterey jack, diced	19.98 g	16.16 g	0.45 g
1 tbsp. olive oil	13.5 g	0 g	0 g
1/2 cup feta, crumbled	15.96 g	10.66 g	3.07 g

Nutrition Facts

Amount	% Daily Value*	Amount	% Daily Value*
Total Fat 60.2g	93%	**Total Carbohydrates** 8g	3%
Saturated 27.4g	137%	Dietary Fiber 3g	10%
Trans Fat 0g		Sugars 5g	
Cholesterol 131mg	44%	**Protein** 30g	59%
Sodium 1205mg	50%		
Calcium 93% • **Iron** 13%		**Vitamin A** 43% • **Vitamin C** 61%	

Amount per 284 g
1 serving (10 oz)

Calories 685
From fat 532

* Percent Daily Values are based on 2000 calorie diet. Your Daily Values may be higher or lower depending on your calorie needs.

Directions:

1.   Prepare a pot of boiling salted water.

2.   Blanch the broccoli and cauliflower for exactly 1 minute. Submerge them immediately in ice water after. Strain on a colander and set aside.

3.   In a large bowl, combine the broccoli, cauliflower, red onion, Monterey jack, feta, olive oil, and red vinegar. Sprinkle the feta on top of the salad.

4.   Toss the salad thoroughly. Serve immediately.

Did you know?

Broccoli rabe may reduce the number of visits to your derm. The phytochemicals and antioxidants found in green veggies like broccoli rabe can help protect your skin against UV damage by countering free radicals in your body to lessen the deterioration of skin's vital components like collagen and elastin. Say hello to greens and say hello to gorgeous skin!

Avocado and Lime Coleslaw

INGREDIENTS	Fats	Proteins	Carbs
1/4 cup red cabbage, shredded	0.04 g	0.32 g	1.64 g
1/4 cup green cabbage, shredded	0.02 g	0.29 g	1.29 g
1/4 cup cilantro	0.02 g	0.09 g	0.15 g
1/4 cup avocado, sliced	5.35 g	0.73 g	3.11 g
1 tbsp. lime juice	0.01 g	0.06 g	1.27 g
1/4 tbsp. garlic, chopped	0 g	0.04 g	0.23 g
1 tbsp. mayonnaise	4.77 g	0.89 g	0.46 g
1 1/2 tbsp. avocado oil	21 g	0g	0 g
1 tbsp. buttermilk	0.13 g	0.51 g	0.73 g
1 tbsp. blue cheese, crumbled	2.3 g	1.71 g	0.19 g
1 1/2 tbsp. olive oil	20.3 g	0 g	0 g

Nutrition Facts

Amount per 181 g
1 serving (6.4 oz)

Calories 524
From fat 475

Amount	% Daily Value*	Amount	% Daily Value*
Total Fat 54g	83%	Total Carbohydrates 9g	3%
Saturated 8g	40%	Dietary Fiber 4g	15%
Trans Fat 0g		Sugars 3g	
Cholesterol 7mg	2%	Protein 5g	9%
Sodium 252mg	11%		
Calcium 10% • Iron 4%		Vitamin A 13% • Vitamin C 51%	

* Percent Daily Values are based on 2000 calorie diet. Your Daily Values may be higher or lower depending on your calorie needs.

Directions:

1.   In a microwave-safe bowl, combine the buttermilk and blue cheese. Microwave the mixture on high for 20 seconds.

2.   To the same bowl, add the avocado oil, olive oil, garlic, lime juice, and mayonnaise. Whisk together until thoroughly mixed.

3.   Add the avocado and mash it in with a fork.

4.   In a large bowl, combine the red cabbage, green cabbage, and cilantro.

5.   Drizzle the dressing all over the salad and toss to mix.

6.   Serve immediately.

Did you know?

Avocados contain more fat than any other fruit or vegetable. Also, the trees contain enzymes that prevent the fruit from ever ripening on the tree, allowing farmers to use the trees as storage devices for up to 7 months after they reach full maturity, allowing avocados to always be in season

FREE E-BOOK

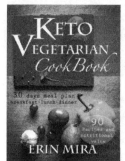 

Congratulations for taking the first step to a keto vegetarian lifestyle!
As a support to your decision, I'm pleased to give you for free the e-book version of this paperback
SUBSCRIBE AND GET FREE EBOOK

https://mailchi.mp/80d2ba48b381/erinmiraketov egetariancookbook

- **Just click the cover image**
- **Follow the link**
- **Scan the code**

If you liked the content of this book, please do leave a review. Reviews are really important to new and established authors for it can make or break their career and also I wanted to make sure I can give you as much quality in my next books..
Thank you again!

Please subscribe to be updated for more vegetarian based books!

THANK YOU !!

KETO VEGETARIAN
BOOKS SERIES

 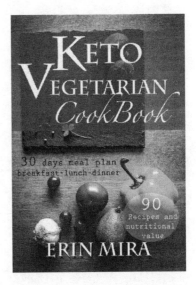

SUBSCRIBE FOR DISCOUNTS AND
PROMOS ON THE NEXT BOOK

THANK YOU!

Made in the USA
San Bernardino, CA
27 December 2018